"Integrating insights from years of practice as a psychotherapist and as a spiritual director, Sue Magrath provides rich content and a healing spirit to *My Burden Is Light: A Primer for Clergy Wellness*. Because of her experience working with so many clergy, her words have the ring of authenticity and practical applicability. She knows what pastors have to deal with and she speaks directly to them about their role and to their soul. Magrath knows that pastoral ministry in the local church is a tough job; she also knows there are resources and strategies clergy often fail to utilize, including retreats, scripture, companions, and counselors. I believe this is a realistic and helpful book that will help many pastors."

—**Jerry P. Haas**, co-author, *The Cycle of Grace: Living in Sacred Balance*

"This is a book that will earn a permanent place on my bookshelf; I only wish I'd had it as I entered ministry! Magrath, grounded in both spiritual direction and psychotherapy and experienced in the local church, deftly leads us through the various areas that affect clergy wellness. Practical and provocative, I can see turning to it on a regular basis to provide the 'how am I doing personally?' check-in that often gets neglected in the busy life of a pastor. This would be an excellent choice for clergy groups providing mutual support and accountability."

—**Mary K. (Sellon) Huycke**, co-author, *Pathway to Renewal*

"Sue Magrath's commitment to clergy wellness shines in this heartfelt, insightful, and very practical book. She effectively combines relevant information with personal reflection. Readers will feel deeply cared for while exploring this book. I was grateful to encounter a wise leader who writes not only from experience, but with great compassion and respect for clergy and all spiritual leaders. This book is truly a gift."

—**Lara Bolger**, Chair of the Board of Ordained Ministry for the Pacific Northwest Annual Conference of the United Methodist Church

My Burden Is Light

My Burden Is Light

A Primer for Clergy Wellness

Sue Magrath

CASCADE *Books* · Eugene, Oregon

MY BURDEN IS LIGHT
A Primer for Clergy Wellness

Cascade Books
An Imprint of Wipf and Stock Publishers
199 W. 8th Ave., Suite 3
Eugene, OR 97401

www.wipfandstock.com

PAPERBACK ISBN: 978-1-5326-8824-9
HARDCOVER ISBN: 978-1-5326-8825-6
EBOOK ISBN: 978-1-5326-8826-3

Cataloguing-in-Publication data:

Names: Magrath, Sue, author.

Title: My burden is light : a primer for clergy wellness / by Sue Magrath.

Description: Eugene, OR: Cascade Books, 2019 | Includes bibliographical references.

Identifiers: ISBN 978-1-5326-8824-9 (paperback) | ISBN 978-1-5326-8825-6 (hardcover) | ISBN 978-1-5326-8826-3 (ebook)

Subjects: LCSH: Clergy—Psychology | Clergy—Heath and hygene | Pastoral care | Religious leaders

Classification: BV4398 M347 2019 (print) | BV4398 (ebook)

Manufactured in the U.S.A.   10/02/19

For all the pastors in my life who nourished the God spark in me and helped set me on this lifelong journey of the Spirit. I am forever in your debt.

"Come to me, all you that are weary and are carrying heavy burdens, and I will give you rest. Take my yoke upon you, and learn from me; for I am gentle and humble in heart, and you will find rest for your souls. For my yoke is easy, and my burden is light."

—MATT 11: 28–30

Contents

Acknowledgments

Though writing is often perceived as a solitary occupation, I think most authors are aware that they are accompanied by angels—those people who encourage, support, and sustain them on this journey of birthing a book. Here are a few of mine.

First of all, I am eternally grateful to my former spiritual director, Suzanne Seaton. Shortly after the acceptance of my first book for publication (which I expected to be a once-in-a-lifetime deal), she asked me this simple question, "What would it mean if you named writing as your primary identity and vocation?" This question wouldn't let me go, and within a week, the genesis of this book took shape.

Other angels include my first supervisor as a therapist, Reverend Eldon Brown, who taught me to trust myself, to be present to the stories of others, and to be curious; my sister, who shared so much of her pastoral journey with me and dared to be vulnerable and honest about the life of clergy; and all the clergy I worked with over the years as a therapist, spiritual director, or colleague who gave me a glimpse of both the struggles and joys of clergy life. I am so grateful to them all.

Thanks go out to Derek McGuckin, whose wonderful experience of swimming with seals made the chapter on sacred play come alive. I was also blessed to have three experienced and insightful clergy friends—Meredith Dodd, Brad Beeman, and J. T. Greenleaf—who took valuable time away from their pastoring duties to read my first draft and be completely honest with me about what they thought. Their comments and suggestions made this a better book. Thank you so much! I'm also grateful to Sherri Wills, who did some last-minute editing that smoothed previously unnoticed rough spots.

I was extremely fortunate to work with some amazing people on the Clergy Wellness Task Force for the Pacific Northwest Conference of the United Methodist Church. Their willingness to spend two years digging into the hard questions and heavy work of seeking to nourish the clergy of our conference was inspiring and gratifying. It was good and fruitful work, and I learned so much from all of them—Willem Romeijn, Denise McGuiness, Carol Tinney, Sam Geyer, Dave Richardson, Meredith Dodd, Brad Beeman, and Daniel Flahiff.

The writing life can be tedious and intense, and the need for respite is real. Fortunately, I am blessed with children and grandchildren who call me back to the real world on a regular basis, reminding me that living in the moment is the best remedy for a fatigued brain. Playing with grandkids might be the most fun it is possible to have in this world. So to Megan, Shauna, Payton, Cullen, Brian, Kelly, and Liam, thank you! You keep me sane.

Finally, I couldn't have done any of this without my husband. His support has been my lifeline. He gives me space when I need it, does the grocery shopping when I am elbow deep in writing, celebrates the successes with me, trumpets my accomplishments to anyone willing to listen, keeps track of my finances, and pulls me away from the computer when my brain is fried. I know there's more that he does behind the scenes that even I don't see. Tom, thank you from the bottom of my heart for all you do for me. You are my chief angel, and I love you forever.

Introduction

My first relationship with a pastor took place during my childhood years in a small-town mainline Protestant church in Northeastern Washington. His name was James Boyd,[1] and I may have had a bit of a schoolgirl crush on him. He was a good-looking man, but what I loved most about him was his kindness, his smile, his way of making me feel like I was important. One Christmas, he helped me surprise my parents with a flute solo during the annual Christmas pageant. Imagine my thrill at having this man whom I revered join me in the subterfuge, helping me concoct the plan to hide my flute up the sleeve of my angel costume so my parents wouldn't see it until the last possible moment. The Boyd's became friends of the family, coming to our home for dinner often, until, as pastors do, they moved on to another church.

My parents stayed in touch with them, but by that time, my interest was on other things, and I didn't think much about Pastor Jim for several years. Then, when I was in high school, we got word that he had had an affair with another woman in the church he was serving, resulting in the break-up of his marriage. His ex-wife moved to the town where we were then living and began attending our church. Jan was crushed, and I remember wondering what on earth could have happened to cause this man, who I had known as kind and loving, to do something that could cause such pain to his wife and family. Today, after many years of relationships with clergy, both personally and professionally, I think I have a better grasp of how easily things can go so terribly wrong.

My entire life has been spent in the church, and pastors have always been some of my favorite people. While I did consider going into the

1. All names changed.

ministry myself a time or two, ultimately I realized that this was not my call. Instead, I entered graduate school at the age of thirty-seven to get a master's degree in counseling. It was hardly a coincidence that my first job upon graduation was with a pastoral counseling agency. Many of my colleagues were clergy, and I developed a number of relationships with other clergy in the area to establish referral sources. I also saw pastors as clients. This was the beginning of my education on the clergy life—its joys and sorrows, its challenges and frustrations. I soon realized the toll ministry took on pastors due to the long hours, impossible expectations, and constant disruptions to a normal family life when called away to pastoral emergencies.

A few years into my therapy career, my sister decided to enter the ministry, and she became yet another window into clergy life. I grew accustomed to her phone calls, wanting to consult on a situation where my mental health knowledge was needed, or sometimes just to vent. She was not immune to the ways in which ministry can wear one down. In other words, she struggled. My sister is six years older than me, and I had always viewed her as something of a Superwoman. She has a large measure of our father's toughness in her, so I couldn't imagine how difficult it would be for pastors who did not possess those same reserves of strength and fortitude.

Another experience that added to my insight into the life of clergy was my enrollment in the Academy for Spiritual Formation, an ecumenical two-year spirituality program offered by the Upper Room of the United Methodist Church. At least half of the people in my cohort were clergy. During those two years, I developed lasting friendships with many of them. The program called us into deep conversations with one another, and this kind of intimate engagement further informed my understanding of the challenges clergy face. I witnessed first-hand the brokenness that many brought with them into ministry, as well as the brokenness that arises out of toxic church experiences and impaired parishioners, colleagues, and superiors. It was here that I first felt the stirring of my passion for clergy wellness.

I later became a spiritual director and had many clergy persons as directees. Listening to their spiritual struggles added yet another dimension to my understanding. Lack of time for prayer or other spiritual practices, doubts about their own faith, difficulty in discerning God's call—all of these issues and more were shared with me in our times together. Ultimately, I left the mental health field entirely to focus more on clergy wellness workshops and retreats, as well as my growing spiritual direction practice.

I continued to maintain my license however, just in case I ever needed a fall-back. This meant that I still had to fulfill continuing education requirements—never my favorite thing. However, as I was surfing the website of an online continuing education provider one day, I came across a course entitled *Clergy Stress and Depression*. I was excited to find a course I was actually interested in that might be of value in my current vocation. I signed up immediately and downloaded the course materials, and what I read over the next few days blew me away. The statistics cited by the authors were alarming.

It started with the fact that 60 to 80 percent of clergy don't remain in ministry more than ten years.[2] In addition, over 77 percent of pastors regularly consider leaving the ministry. Later, when I presented these statistics to a large group of clergy, they chuckled. I took that to mean this was no surprise to them. But as a mental health professional, I was even more alarmed by some of the other statistics—70 percent come from dysfunctional homes, and only 32 percent of those had ever sought any kind of counseling to work on those issues; 75 percent have experienced one or more episodes of depression; and the rate of alcoholism among clergy is between two and four times the national average.

Armed with these statistics and more, I scheduled a meeting with the chair of our denomination's Board of Ordained Ministry. It turned out he had the same concerns as I and had just begun thinking about how to approach the problem in our conference. The result of our conversation was a two-year task force on clergy wellness, which I chaired. This task force met monthly to discuss the full scope of the problem, identify all the areas of life that are impacted, and sometimes compromised, by ministry in the church. We made recommendations to the Board about how they could begin to create a culture of wellness in our conference. As a result of this task force, a number of new programs were implemented, and resources were identified and made available to conference clergy. It was toward the end of this two-year journey that I felt the call to write this book. Readers will find in these pages all that I have learned over a lifetime of relationships with clergy, formal education, and professional experience. Grounded in psychological knowledge, spiritual insight, and personal engagement, my desire is that readers will discover hope, comfort, and real, practical guidance to light their way as they seek to be faithful to God's call on their lives to shepherd God's people.

2. Gauger and Christie, *Clergy Stress*, 2.

1

Self-Care

The Essential Ingredient

Jacob's well was there, and Jesus, tired as he was from the journey, sat down by the well. It was about the sixth hour. When a Samaritan woman came to draw water, Jesus said to her, "Will you give me a drink?"

—John 4:6–7 (NIV)

The life of ministry is not just a job or career, it is a vocation. It goes beyond a means of making a living to being an identity, something that defines you and gives your life meaning. Serving the church is an overwhelming obligation at the best of times, and it is a commitment that is indefinable and elusively difficult to quantify. There is nothing "nine to five" about the ministry. The people of your flock need you when they need you, and church emergencies are no respecter of office hours. It is not surprising to discover that many clergy are working as many as sixty hours a week or more in order to keep up with the many demands of the church. Worship planning and sermon preparation, pastoral visits, committee meetings, long-range visioning, small-group preparation and leadership, phone calls, community outreach, and administrative duties are just some of the tasks that are expected of pastors. Add to that the expectations of the larger church—membership in broader church committees, participation in clergy cluster groups, and fulfilling the requirements for accountability to superiors. There is never a time when the to-do list is completed. And for those who feel they can't take time for themselves until their tasks are done, this creates a huge problem. Self-care becomes just another item on the list that continually moves to the bottom in favor of other higher priority needs. The problem is that by the time a pastor's lack of well-being becomes an emergency, it is often too late for minor adjustments or a couple of hours a week devoted to self-care to make a difference.

One of the metaphors that I often hear used to illustrate the need for self-care is the injunction offered by flight attendants on an airplane encouraging parents to put their own oxygen mask on first before assisting their children. In other words, you need to breathe in the vital oxygen before you fall unconscious and are then unable to give oxygen to those who are dependent on you. It's a good reminder, but unfortunately this metaphor breaks down when you examine it more closely. In ministry, nobody is going to dangle an oxygen mask in front of you and tell you that you are in trouble. Churches are often so focused on their own needs that they are not paying attention to the well-being of their pastor. They are not taking you aside to ask you how you are doing after you have performed ten funerals in the past year. They are not urging you to take more vacation days or a regular Sabbath. They are not telling you that it's okay to skip a committee meeting every once in a while. They are not likely to notice if you are depressed or exhausted or burned out.

And the truth is that the clergy person might not notice it either. Burn-out is a gradual and insidious process. It's a little like that proverbial pot of frogs on a stove you've heard about. Because they are cold-blooded, frogs don't even notice when the water in the pot begins to get warmer and warmer because someone turned the burner on. By the time they notice, the water is boiling, and they're already cooked!

So let's consider a different metaphor that is more helpful in considering the need for self-care. Imagine a lovely pond in the woods. The water in the pond is pure and clear. Fish and frogs consider the pond their home, and ducks can rest and find food on their long migrations. Deer and other forest creatures come to drink the cool water, and sometimes children come to play and swim. The pond is a peaceful place where people can picnic or just flop down in the shade for a rest from their labors, experiencing peace and renewal. It is a place of nourishment—physically, emotionally, and spiritually. This pond is you, the clergy person.

Now, think back to your elementary school science class and consider what such a pond might need in order to stay healthy. It needs a source of fresh water—an "in-flow"—and it needs an outlet. This constant cycle of in-flow and out-flow keeps the water refreshed and healthy. Ponds that are fed only by an occasional rainfall and have no outlet will quickly become stagnant or dry up. Ponds with a source that feeds them but has no outlet will overflow and destroy the surrounding terrain. But the biggest danger is that when a pond has no in-flow, the outlet will drain the pond. It will be emptied out with no means to replenish it. For pastors, the outlet is not a problem. There are lots of opportunities every day to share your love of God and others, to care for the people you serve as Jesus commanded, doing for the least of these as you would for Christ. There are so many places where the living water of which you are a vessel is desperately needed to be poured out for the healing of the world. Love and hope and peace are in short supply on this planet we call home, and the life of ministry is about pointing others to the ultimate Source and guiding them on the path toward the Divine.

However, if clergy are too busy pouring themselves out for others, they often fail to maintain the source of in-flow. Research shows that in any given thirty-day period, 28 percent of clergy have not taken a day off, and another 28 percent have only taken one or two days off.[1] When pastors are working this much, it is impossible to make time to receive the renewal they need. They are cutting themselves off from the streams of living water about which Jesus spoke to the Samaritan woman.[2] They fail to stay connected to the spring that refreshes and restores.

So what would that source of in-flow look like for pastors? How do you feed your pond in order to stay healthy? One important way is through life-long learning. This includes continuing education courses, of course, but also classes that develop your other interests and avocations—learning a foreign language, taking photography lessons, or signing up for pottery, fly-fishing, or cooking classes. Pay attention to your own inner longings, and you will discover something you have always wanted to do or learn.

Another way to reconnect with your Source is through regular retreat and Sabbath. Silence and solitude are essential means through which to be in union with God, receiving the peace and insight that God willingly gives when we make ourselves available. The possibilities are endless for finding ways to lovingly care for yourself in the service of others. It's really a matter of good stewardship. Clergy are instruments of God in the

1. Gauger and Christie, *Clergy Stress,* 12.
2. John 4:13.

3

world whose gifts need to be nurtured and maintained in order to do the work to which they are called.

Self-care is about the nourishment of every aspect of the self. It is simply, at its core, about balance. In fact, our earliest spiritual teachers taught that holiness is not achieved through piety but through balance. Certainly, Scripture supports this idea of balance. When Jesus is questioned by the teacher of the law about which commandment was the most important, he answered, "Love the Lord your God with all your heart and with all your soul and with all your mind and with all your strength."[3] It seems that Jesus is suggesting that when we bring our whole self to God—the emotional, spiritual, mental, and physical aspects of ourselves in equal measure—then we are living into the completeness and Oneness of God. It is only when we are whole that we are able to minister to others in a healthy way. The words "whole" and "health" both come from the same Old English word "haelan," which means to cure, save, or make whole. These words are at the heart of this concept we call clergy wellness.

Throughout this book, we will explore all of these aspects of self that are often lacking attention and care with some fun and interesting side trips along the way. You will find many ideas for nourishing your mind, body, and spirit and replenishing the metaphorical pond. And you will learn the importance of creating a support network of family, friends, colleagues, and helping professionals who can partner with you in your journey to health and wholeness.

Reflection Questions

1. Think of a time when your energy for ministry was at low ebb. What were the factors that contributed to your weariness and discouragement?

2. What are the things you are currently doing for self-care? When you write them down, does it look and feel like enough?

3. What are your yearnings? What are you thirsty for? How to get there is for another day. For now, it is enough to identify those places where you are experiencing a deep longing.

3. Mark 12:30.

2

Solitude

The Crucible of the Soul

But Jesus often withdrew to lonely places and prayed.

—Luke 5:16 (NIV)

M any years ago, I was a pastoral counselor approaching burnout. I was in deep need of re-charging my soul and had planned a weekend alone at my cabin in the woods. When I told my spiritual director of my plans, she handed me a little book by Henri Nouwen entitled *Out of Solitude*. Her gesture proved to be a wise one, as the book was just what I needed. Nouwen's book reminded me again of something I've always known, that solitude is the balancing act to the extreme engagement with the world that we call ministry. Nouwen talks about how often Jesus went to a lonely place to pray and how important that was to his ministry, that it was the source of his courage, his unity with the Creator, and his presence with others. Nouwen writes:

> Somewhere we know that without silence words lose their meaning, that without listening speaking no longer heals, that without distance closeness cannot cure. Somewhere we know that without a lonely place our actions quickly become empty gestures. The careful balance between silence and words, withdrawal and involvement, distance and closeness, solitude and community forms the basis of the Christian life.[1]

1. Nouwen, *Out of Solitude*, 14.

The dictionary defines solitude as "seclusion, isolation, or remoteness; a lonely or secluded place."[2] Put that way, solitude might scare some people off. We are a culture that seems almost terrified of being alone and goes to great lengths to avoid it. There is an apocryphal story about Carl Jung that was told frequently in my graduate counseling program. The story goes that a middle-aged gentleman came to Jung complaining of his terror of being alone. At the end of his first session, Jung recommended that the man spend one full hour every day in solitude. The following week, the man returned for his session, and Jung asked how his assignment had turned out. The man exclaimed, "I found out that I can't stand myself!" to which Jung replied, "See what you're inflicting on the rest of us?"

This is the scary part, that we might not like what we discover when we enter the lonely place. Solitude and silence are the crucible of soul work. It can be troubling, frightening even, to expose our souls to God in this way. And yet, how can we minister from a place of true self unless we know what our true self is? Dwight Moody once said, "Character is what you are in the dark."[3] I would paraphrase that to say that true self is who you are when you are alone in the dark. Thomas Merton writes, "He who attempts to act and do things for others or for the world without deepening his own self-understanding, freedom, integrity and capacity to love, will not have anything to give others."[4] It is in solitude that we enter into that voyage of self-discovery.

Several years ago, as I was in the process of closing my therapy practice and moving to another state, I felt an urgent need to go on a silent directed retreat in order to relinquish my identity as a psychotherapist. I made the arrangements for a four-day stay at a retreat center near the ocean in San Diego. Something about the wide-open expanse of the sea seemed to call to me as a place of self-emptying. Shortly after I arrived, I met with my assigned spiritual director to explain my goal for the time away. When I shared that I needed to let go of my role as therapist, she paused for a moment. Then she said, "I think it might be advisable to let go of *all* your roles for a few days. When you strip yourself of these pieces of identity before God, you allow God to do the work of revealing your essence, which will guide your choice of which roles to pick back up again." I followed this wise advice and found the practice to be immensely helpful as I pondered what was next for me. I

2. *Merriam-Webster Dictionary*, 693.

3 Halloran, "Moody Quotes" (website).

4. Merton, *Seeds*, 131.

read a little, listened into the silence, wrote copious questions and insights in my journal, and walked the beach for hours. And I noticed that the first piece of identity to come back "online" was writing. I came to a place of peace about my decision to walk away from the counseling profession, and I felt an assurance that God still had plans for me. I believe that this kind of silent, solitary contemplation is essential to the life of ministry in whatever context it is lived out. It restores us to God, and it restores us to ourselves. When we are truly at home with ourselves, we are better able to be present to others, to create a safe sanctuary for them.

Solitude is also the correction to enmeshment and codependency. It is so easy for clergy to get caught up in the need to be needed, to only feel real or important if we are helping others, responding to their neediness no matter what else we have going on, answering the urgent phone call in the middle of the night. Our self-esteem becomes contingent upon doing good, being the care-giver, the shoulder to cry on, the person everyone turns to in times of trouble. We lose our sense of healthy boundaries and take on the problems of others as if they were our own. But it is in solitude that we remember this is *God's* work, not ours, that our worth is not the same as our usefulness, and that our significance to God is not about what we do, but about who we are. When we are alone, we are stripped of the roles by which the world defines us, and we rediscover our identity as a child of God. At the same time as we reclaim a worth that is not based on accomplishment, we also remember to be humble and let our ego-self take a back seat in our encounter with the great "I am." When we are less driven by our own ideas, plans, and desires, there is room for the Holy Spirit to be the energy behind our vocation and ministry.

Another benefit of solitude is rest and renewal. One of my favorite prayers is this one from the Book of Common Prayer: "O God of peace, You have taught us that in returning and rest we shall be saved, in quietness and confidence shall be our strength. By the might of your Spirit lift us, we pray, to your presence, where we may be still and know that you are God."[5] In this place of returning and rest, we renew our relationship with God and are restored by God's nurturing love. God calls us to return to God's self again and again. When we are with God, there is nothing to do, no list to consult; we can allow bodies and souls to relax and immerse ourselves in the presence of the Beloved. Our senses come alive and energy returns, readying us to move out into the world again. Sue Monk Kidd writes, "Solitude brings me back

---

5. *Book of Common Prayer*, "For Quiet Confidence," 832.

to a simplicity of spirit, an inner poverty that I need in order to clear room inside. It allows me to empty myself out, so there is gracious space within where I can receive myself, then God, and eventually others."[6]

In solitude, we also heal our relationship with time. In our daily lives, we are slaves to the clock, to *chronos*, which is marked and measured. Our hours are dictated by our day planner, our to-do list, and all the tasks that must be squeezed in between one meeting and the next. We have lost touch with *kairos*, or kingdom time, when time does not consist of hours and minutes but the eternal flow of the Spirit, which transcends time, when the coming of the kingdom is happening right now, and we are a part of it.

Years ago, I regularly hired a Swedish gentleman with a strong accent to clean my carpets. His children and mine were in the same grades in school, and his wife was a friend, so we chatted often when he was in my home. One day while he was there, I was getting ready to leave for an important meeting, and I was rushing around the house gathering the things I would need to take with me. As I scurried past him, he chided me with these words, "Yoost (sic) slow down. All the time I been knowing you, you are always in a hurry!" That got my attention! It has been twenty years ago since that day, and I can still hear his voice in that slow, accented English, as though he were standing right next to me.

I think my Swedish friend, Anders, would resonate with the Amish concept of "slow time"—time that is unregulated and responds to the movement of the Holy Spirit. Slow time is not so much a speed but a state of mind, a way of living intentionally. It is about being aware of self and others in the present moment so that we might respond from the Christ within rather than the cultural dictates of a world that is rushing headlong into nothingness. In the introduction to her Merton compilation, *Book of Hours*, Kathleen Deignan says:

> We have made time a problem, and our language betrays how yet another living mystery has become a commercial commodity to make, take, give, lose, spend, save, share, waste, beat, stretch, manage, and kill. . . . There is no room for the mysterious spaciousness of being, no time for presence; no room for nature, no time for quiet, for thought, for presence.[7]

---

6. Kidd, *Firstlight*, 88.

7. Merton, *Book of Hours*, 32.

I believe it is in solitude that we enter into God's time, when breath and heartbeat find their natural rhythm and resonate with the rhythms of the universe. It is where we reclaim our own soul.

Solitude is also a place in which to discover perspective. Wisdom requires enough space for us to pay attention to God and our own inner knowing. Solitude removes the distractions of our lives and allows us to see things more clearly. We can examine the situations in which we find ourselves and notice patterns of interaction that might not be healthy. We can see possible solutions that don't often come when we are deep in the midst of a problem or conflict. In solitude, we find a healthy distance that allows us to hear and hold the suffering of others without becoming so absorbed in it that we can't find the boundary between their suffering and our own. It is where we realize that we cannot do another person's suffering for them. It is where we can look at our current situations from the long view, in light of our own history and God's story, our stories of both trial and blessing, and find the hope that is often apparent when we see the hand of God working in our past and our present.

As you begin to experience for yourself the blessings of solitude, you might be tempted to become a monastic. At times, ministry might find you longing for the cloistered walls of a monastery from which you rarely venture forth. But I doubt that would be true to your call to ministry. Solitude is merely one part of an inward and outward movement that feeds us and then enables us to feed the other. Howard Rice writes, "We move back and forth between being renewed in silence and quiet by ourselves . . . and then carrying that new energy out into the world with vigor. This back-and-forth pattern is a central way in which the spiritual experience of the individual is related to the activity of the disciple."[8] If you look at the example of Christ, you can see that this is the pattern of his own ministry as well. Shortly after I had completed the Academy for Spiritual Formation and was about to embark on a ministry of spiritual direction, my own spiritual director reminded me of the story of Jesus walking on water as told in Mark 5:30–52. She asked me what I thought it would take to have that kind of balance, inner stillness, and presence to walk with people through the storms of their lives without drowning myself. This drew me into a deeper study of that passage, and it revealed some important insights for me and for anyone who is called to ministry.

8. Job and Shawchuck, *Guide to Prayer*, 327.

If you start with the scene immediately before, you can see the cycle of the inward and outward movements that Jesus exemplified. It starts with an outward movement, the feeding of the five thousand. Imagine for a moment how draining that was. Thousands of people gathered around Jesus, eager for his message, clamoring for his attention, his touch, his healing miracles. Jesus was a pretty hands-on kind of guy, so I'm sure he walked among them while teaching, blessing, and healing. I'd guess it was a little more taxing than your usual Sunday service! And then, he performed the miracle of the loaves and fishes, God's abundant provision for God's people. I have to believe it takes a lot of energy to perform a miracle, so afterwards he must have been spent.

Next comes the inward movement: "Immediately Jesus made the disciples get into the boat and go on ahead of him to the other side, while he dismissed the crowd. After he had dismissed them, he went up on a mountainside by himself to pray,"[9] This was the renewal that Jesus needed, the restorative to such intense engagement with God's people, the sheep in need of a shepherd. One of the key points in this passage is how long Jesus stayed on that mountain. There are actually clues in the text that help us determine that. It says from evening (which could mean anywhere from about six to eight PM, but definitely before or right at sunset in order for him to still be able to see the boat floundering on the lake) until the fourth watch, which is between three AM and sunrise. This means that for a minimum of seven hours, Jesus allowed the disciples to battle their own storm. *They were struggling, and he let them!* He wasn't going to let them die, but he needed those hours of solitude and rest before he could re-engage with the troubles of the world (the outward movement). He needed to find his inner still point in order to walk on stormy seas and be fully present to calm the disciples' fears.

This is why I believe that *solitude is the single most essential element of self-care.* It is what makes pastors better able to be present to the world, to their congregations, to the suffering ones, to their families and friends. It is what restores your souls and allows you to keep going, to keep doing the work of ministry, the work of bringing about God's kingdom on earth. Think about the difference in you when you are on your last nerve versus when you have had the chance to spend time alone with God.

The challenge is trying to fit solitude into your busy schedule, especially if you are the parent of school-age children or have care-giving

9. Mark 6: 45–46 (NIV).

responsibilities for aging parents or other family members. When this is the case, even an hour of solitude might be more than you can spare, but that's okay. Sometimes just a few minutes can be enough to restore your batteries. Some possible opportunities might be the time you spend waiting while your child has soccer practice or piano lessons, et cetera. Take advantage of that time to walk around the block or find a chair or bench that is in a different room or outside. Find a tree to sit under. If you are visiting a parishioner in the hospital, take a quick detour into the chapel for ten minutes of centering prayer. If you have a dog, go outside when you let him or her out for the final time at night, gaze at the stars and breathe in the fresh air. Enjoy a few moments of peace and quiet. If a meeting or appointment gets cancelled, fight the tendency to use that time for catching up on church work. Drive to a local park or sit in the silence of your own sanctuary instead.

For those who are able, scheduling longer periods of time for silence will be worth the effort in terms of peace of mind, strength of will, and the ability to be fully present to others. Try it for an hour a week, then maybe a half-day every month, then for a full day, perhaps once a quarter. At some point, you might feel compelled to go on a two- or three-day silent retreat. Your congregation might flounder as the disciples did, but it won't sink without you. And once you set an intention for this important soul work, the door to *kairos* time will open up and invite you in.

Reflection Questions

1. What is your current practice of solitude and silence?

2. What are the internal barriers to creating more space for solitude?

3. What are the benefits you have received from past experiences of solitude?

4. What would it take for you to begin setting aside time for this renewing spiritual practice?

3

Kryptonite I

Unearthing Your Emotional Wounds

Even if my father and mother abandon me, the LORD will hold me close.

—PSALM 27:10 (NLT)

We all have our kryptonite—that area of vulnerability, the Achilles heel that we hope will never catch up with us. But it does—sometimes in the most inconvenient times and places. Especially for clergy. What am I talking about? I'm referring to the emotional wounds of childhood or other painful events from the past that hang around, lurking in a dark corner of your psyche long into adulthood. If unaddressed, these wounds can make you vulnerable to people and situations that stir up long-denied feelings and unhealthy coping mechanisms.

We are all wounded. It is not possible to escape the bonds of human life without having received some scars along the way. In fact, research into the stressors of clergy life has found that approximately 70 percent of clergy come from dysfunctional families of origin.[1] Of those, only one third have ever sought counseling to resolve the issues of that early childhood pain.[2] It should come as no surprise then that life in the church, often with comparable relationships and dynamics to family life, has the potential to open up those old wounds and create new problems, limiting one's ability to function appropriately when events trigger old patterns.

1. London and Wiseman, *Pastors at Greater Risk*, 45.
2. Gauger and Christie, *Clergy Stress*, 22.

12

The first step in any process of healing is acknowledging and naming one's wounds. As Flora Slosson Wuellner puts it, "Little can change until we have faced where we actually are."[3] There are many, many different types of wounds, and some of them might not even be recognized as wounds until you pay attention to how they make you feel and how they have impacted your life. Some possible wounds clergy might have experienced include the death of a friend, family member, or significant other; a betrayal by family, friends, or co-workers; divorce or infidelity of a partner; job loss; addiction (self or others); neglect or abandonment; physical, sexual, or emotional abuse; personal injury, illness, or disability; problems with children due to rebellion or mental illness; toxic or dysfunctional churches. This is by no means an exhaustive list, but it can serve as a way to begin identifying those painful people, episodes, or abuses that have played a part in creating the wounds we bear.

As you read through the remainder of this chapter, you might want to highlight or underline passages that relate to your experiences, maybe jotting down notes or questions in the margins. Keep your journal nearby so that you can write down memories that may have been stirred up, concepts that resonate with you, or any insights you receive about past events that are impacting current situations or behavior. Give yourself permission to set the book aside for a while if you need time to assimilate new understandings or painful emotions. At the end of the chapter, I will invite you to dig deeper into these personal revelations.

Family Dynamics

Family—they can be our greatest blessing and the source of our deepest pain. We love them, we hate them, we long for connection, and we need to get away from them, sometimes all at the same time. But I think it's safe to say that everyone at one time or another has spoken aloud the words, "My family makes me crazy!" And they do. Being with family is like being caught up in the middle of a rushing river. You are carried along on the current of how families do relationships, and it's very difficult to see those patterns until you step out of the river and observe them from afar. It is my hope to help you do that by introducing some concepts from the counseling world, particularly in the area of family systems theory.

3. Wuellner, *Forgiveness, the Passionate Journey,* 26.

Looking at the family as a system helps to make sense of patterns of behavior and their purpose. In any family, the purpose is to maintain the status quo, commonly referred to as homeostasis. It works a little like a thermostat to regulate the temperature in your home. If the temperature in the house goes lower than the set point, the thermostat automatically turns up the heat until the desired temperature is attained, at which point it turns off again. All members of a family have designated though usually unspoken roles. When each member behaves in their usual manner, all is as it should be. (This does not mean that it's healthy, just that it is normative for a particular family. This could be highly conflictual or dysfunctional, but it is the family set point.) However, if any one member of the family attempts to alter the dynamic, the thermostat kicks on, and pressure is put to bear on that person to get back into line playing their assigned part in the family system.

There are many different dimensions of family dynamics. One of those dimensions is the continuum of connection, from enmeshed on one end of the spectrum to disconnected and distant at the other end. Some families are so close, it's like they are living in each other's pockets. Boundaries are non-existent, and everybody has to know everybody else's business. Some examples of an enmeshed family are a mother who texts her children several times a day and freaks out if they fail to respond in a timely manner or a family in which members are expected to do everything together. Children who want to go away to university rather than attend the local community college have to endure endless histrionics about them stepping out on their own. Healthy individuation is not valued and is actively discouraged.

On the other hand, a distant family has very little connection. The expression of affection is scarce; there is a minimum of conversation at the dinner table; parents seldom attend their children's school and/or sporting events; and a feeling of genuine connection between parents and adult children is rare. Children from these families can feel neglected, ignored, and invisible. Of course, cultural norms are also at play here, and one may have grown up in either of these two extremes and considered it completely normal. If you grew up in a minority culture, you may not view one or the other of these patterns to be dysfunctional and did not perceive your upbringing to be painful in any way.

When a person grows up in either of these extreme ends of the spectrum of connection, one can see how that might impact their ability to relate to others in healthy ways, particularly as a pastor in a church setting. Most clergy (and their congregants) tend to view the church as a big family, even if this goes largely unacknowledged. Therefore, they may unconsciously attempt to replicate the unhealthy patterns of childhood without realizing it. For example, a pastor from an enmeshed family might have difficulty in maintaining appropriate boundaries and desire closer relationships to congregants than is healthy or acceptable. And clergy members from distant families might be confused by church members' desires for a sense of connection, empathy, or warmth from their pastor.

While neither of these extremes of family behavior can be described as healthy, they are still to some degree "normal." The families that do the most damage are those that are abusive, either emotionally, physically, sexually, or any combination thereof. Often, these are families in which addiction and/or rage plays a major role and is not limited to substances, as there are many kinds of addiction. Typically, there is one person in the family that is the primary perpetrator of abusive or addictive behavior. By looking at an addiction model of family roles, it is possible to identify the functions of various family members and thus understand the way these dynamics worked to preserve the family system. Once these roles and behaviors have been unmasked, it is possible to recognize unhealthy coping mechanisms and how they play into current behaviors that may have become problematic.

The person in the family who is the addict or abuser is the one around whom all other roles revolve. He or she was likely abused or deeply wounded in childhood and is continuing the family "legacy" into the next generation. While it is extraordinarily difficult to have compassion for the person in your family who is hurting you the most, it is important to understand the source and depth of their pain. While this insight may not lead to forgiveness, it does allow one a different perspective on the wounds that shaped them and may offer a certain measure of healing. We will discuss the idea of forgiveness in the next chapter.

The second major role in this system is the enabler. The enabler is often, but not always, the spouse. This person makes excuses for the addict or abuser, takes care of him or her, assumes the abuser's primary functions around the home, and basically prevents the addict from experiencing any negative consequences for his or her actions. After an episode of drinking, raging, or abuse, the enabler will tend to the children's feelings and try to explain away the behavior with statements like "He didn't mean it" or "She can't help herself." Unfortunately, the enabler's desire to protect the family and help the abuser ends up being counter-productive. Both enabler and addict move deeper into denial through this pattern. The addict/abuser doesn't have to seek help, and the enabler pretends that everything is fine, and the next episode will be different.

Often the oldest child, the star or hero role, works hard to bring positive attention to the family. Such children are overly responsible, hard-working, and achievement oriented. They are usually excellent students, and take on a more adult role in the family, assisting the enabler in caring for younger children as well as offering emotional support to him/her. Sadly, their focus on being the star often leaves them feeling that they have no identity of their own, nor any awareness of their own needs. No matter how hard they try, their efforts are never enough.

In the high conflict and drama of this type of family, there is usually one of the offspring that is a lost child. This is the one who falls through the cracks, who withdraws and keeps a low profile in order to avoid getting hurt. They learn how to avoid drawing attention to themselves as a defense mechanism, which can also leave them feeling ignored, invisible, and unloved.

Another role is the scapegoat. This is the child who acts out as a result of the family dysfunction and therefore gets blamed for the family problems. This is often the only way a family will get help. They bring the scapegoat to a therapist for treatment as the "identified patient," but in the process the true issue may get uncovered, and possibly the person who is the real source of the problems will agree to a treatment program or therapy.

Depending on the family and the number of children, the youngest child often is identified as the mascot. Mascots are cute, cuddly, and entertaining. They are often spoiled and given positive attention. Older siblings, who have been a part of the system for a while, will try to protect the mascot from what is happening and may keep things from him or her so she/he doesn't have to know the painful truth.

Spend a little time with this model, perhaps identifying what role you and your family members took on. What feelings and insights come up for you as you consider how this has impacted your adult life—your relationships, your emotional life, and your ability to function in your ministry setting? How does this change the way you view yourself, your siblings, and your parents? Do you see ways in which you have replicated certain aspects of your family of origin in your current family? Talk to your loved ones about this new understanding. If you are able to communicate with your siblings, contact them to share what you have learned and check their perceptions of the dynamics you experienced in your childhood home. If this stirs up old wounds, seek the help of a therapist well-versed in family dynamics to work through these issues, to find healing, and to facilitate growth into more healthy behaviors and ways of relating to self and others.

Personality Disorders

Often, the people we have the most difficulty with—in our families and in our churches—are people who have personality disorders. Personality disorders are different from other mental disorders in that they affect the personality of the individual and are manifested by pervasive and persistent patterns of thought, behavior, emotion, interpersonal functioning, and impulse control. These disorders are longstanding and resistant to therapeutic intervention. They are not connected to chemical imbalances in the brain or genetic pre-dispositions, therefore medication is not effective unless they also are suffering from anxiety or depression. One of the characteristics of people with these disorders is that they don't believe anything is wrong with them, while the people in their lives often suffer great distress in their relationship with this person. The same roles discussed in the previous section would also apply in a family where one member has a personality disorder. Family members who have been deeply wounded by them are often vulnerable to being hurt by other people they encounter with the same personality disorder. This goes back to the idea of kryptonite. Identifying the particular disorder that a problematic person manifests helps you to know who you will be most vulnerable to in adulthood. For example, I grew up with a narcissistic father, and have therefore been more vulnerable to other narcissists in my adult life. I can enter a room full of strangers, and in fifteen minutes I will have identified all the narcissists so that I can avoid them at all costs!

Awareness and recognition are the key. By learning about personality disorders, you may realize that a parent, sibling, or other person who caused you emotional pain could have this personality disorder. This insight is helpful in several ways. First of all, it helps you to take their behavior less personally. This is who they are, and their actions are not really about you. They are merely responding in the way that their view of self and the world demands in any given situation. When you can recognize their specific patterns of thought, emotion, and behavior, you can begin to respond in more effective ways and even predict and avoid harmful interactions. In addition, understanding the underlying causes of such disorders can help you to have compassion for the person rather than continuing to feel constant hurt, resentment, or anger toward them. This does not mean you have to be their best friend. It will often be necessary for you to set good boundaries and maintain a healthy distance in order to avoid putting yourself in harm's way. Following are brief descriptions of some of the personality disorders most likely to create problems for clergy.

Borderline Personality Disorder

Borderline Personality Disorder is a pattern of instability in interpersonal relationships, self-image, and emotional expression, as well as pronounced impulsivity, which may include suicidal gestures and/or self-harming behaviors. People with Borderline PD have an exaggerated fear of abandonment and engage in frantic efforts to avoid it. Early in relationships, they tend to idealize caregivers, friends, or love interests, but as soon as there is the slightest failure of that person in giving love, care, or attention, the individual dramatically shifts to an extreme devaluation of them. Borderline individuals can be quite impulsive, often engaging in risky behaviors such as gambling, substance abuse, unsafe sex, irresponsible spending, or binge-eating. They are known to engage in suicidal behavior, including threats, gestures, or actual self-harm, which may be perceived as highly manipulative. People with BPD experience an unstable sense of self characterized by shifting goals, values, and vocational plans, often resulting in recurrent job losses, incomplete education, and broken marriages. The individual's emotional reactions can be sudden and extreme, and excessive anger, anxiety, and verbal outbursts are common. Their childhood history often includes physical and/or sexual abuse, neglect, high conflict, and/or early parental loss or separation. Borderlines will complain that you aren't attentive enough or don't love them enough. When things don't go their way, they may seemingly "fall apart" or become very angry. Having a borderline parent can cause one to be either conflict-avoidant or angry as an adult. They may need to exert a high level of control over their environment in response to their chaotic childhood. The roller coaster of emotions takes its toll. A former client of mine had a mother with BPD. She was frequently suicidal, and he recalls an episode when he was in high school in which she locked herself in the bathroom, ran a bath, and held a razor blade to her wrists, narrating each step of her suicide plan.

He ended up having to break down the door in order to prevent her from following through on her threats.

Narcissistic Personality Disorder

Narcissistic Personality Disorder is a pattern of grandiosity, arrogance, extreme need for admiration, and lack of empathy for others. Narcissists are highly egocentric and often have an exaggerated sense of self-importance. They expend a lot of energy on boosting, preserving, and defending their ego, which leads to a deep sensitivity to perceived criticism. They need to be right at all costs. Anything that causes them to feel shame will be met with anger and counterattack. These individuals have a sense of entitlement and are often angry when others fail to meet their expectations. They are typically incapable of empathy, which can make the people in their lives feel unloved and unimportant. The origins of this disorder are usually highly critical and distant parents whose actions create low self-esteem or parents who give the child every material thing they want but withhold love and attention. In order to cover up their perceived flaws, the sufferer creates a façade of self-confidence and superiority. Children of narcissistic parents end up feeling that they don't matter and that their needs are unimportant. It is difficult for them to understand that it is acceptable to have an opinion that is different from their parent.

Histrionic Personality Disorder

Histrionic Personality Disorder is a pattern of excessive emotionality and attention-seeking behavior, such as impressionistic speech, theatrical gestures, and provocative attire. These individuals are usually larger than life, and everything is done with dramatic flair, yet their speech is often without substance. They love to be the center of attention and are upset when they are not. Sometimes it might feel to others that they suck out all the air in the room. Relationships are assumed to be closer than they actually are. People with this disorder crave novelty and excitement and are frustrated by delayed gratification. They are easily influenced by others, changing opinions and emotions at the drop of a hat. There is a tendency to play the victim role and be emotionally manipulative. These are people who didn't get much attention as a child and seek to achieve it in adulthood by means of extreme emotionality and over-the-top dress and language. The offspring of people with HPD often try to fade into the woodwork and often feel deeply embarrassed by their parents' overt attempts to gain attention.

Obsessive-Compulsive Personality Disorder

Obsessive-compulsive Personality Disorder is a pattern of preoccupation with orderliness, perfectionism, and control. Control is achieved by means of painstaking attention to rules, details, procedures, lists, and schedules to the extent that the major point of the activity is lost. Time is poorly allocated, so that tasks often take far more time than they should. These individuals are workaholics with a great need to be productive. They are rigid and inflexible, insisting on strict compliance with rules, morals, and ethics. Those with OCPD are usually quite miserly to the point of self-denial; money is always to be saved for the proverbial rainy day. They have a deep need to be appreciated for what they do. Their parents were often equally perfectionistic, critical, and controlling, teaching the child that there is only one right way to do anything. These children then grow up to have low self-esteem that can only be eased through performing tasks perfectly and following all the rules to the letter.

Dependent Personality Disorder

Dependent Personality Disorder is a pattern of submissive and clinging behavior related to an excessive need to be taken care of. Such individuals suffer from extremely low self-esteem and feel incapable of making everyday decisions. They need excessive amounts of advice and reassurance from others. They are unable to express disagreement for fear of loss of support or approval. Actions are aimed at pleasing others to the point of volunteering for unpleasant tasks, yet their dependence on others makes them unable to initiate projects or work on their own. It is difficult to tolerate the neediness of people like this, and the temptation is to just do things for them. Unfortunately, this is often what they experienced in childhood due to over-anxious and over-protective parents who tended to restrict their activities and do things for them rather than allowing them to learn by trial and error. Children of a dependent parent are often expected to take on adult responsibilities at an early age, having to take care of their parent or siblings before they actually have the requisite skills. This forces them to learn on the fly, which can lead to anxiety and self-doubt. Offspring often end up feeling that it is their job to take care of everyone, which might lead them to overstep boundaries.

Paranoid Personality Disorder

Paranoid Personality Disorder is characterized by deep distrust of others and the assumption that the motives of others are often negative and that their actions were intended to be harmful. People with this disorder continually doubt the loyalty or trustworthiness of friends, family, and work associates. They are highly suspicious and read malicious meanings into even the most benign statements or actions. They bear grudges and are unlikely to forgive insults or injuries despite sincere apology. They assume criticism where none exists, and they are extremely jealous in their intimate relationships, suspecting infidelity even when there is no evidence to support it. They are certainly capable of violence, making it likely that their offspring will have experienced, witnessed, or been traumatized by their aggression. Not surprisingly, this was their experience of childhood as well—a high-conflict environment that included violence and distrust. Children of people with PPD grow up believing that violence and suspicion are a normal part of family life. They may end up becoming a victim or learning that violence is an acceptable way to resolve problems.

Schizoid Personality Disorder

Schizoid Personality Disorder is defined by a detachment from social relationships and a restricted affect. The person with SPD seems to neither desire nor enjoy close relationships, even with family members. They prefer solitary activities and strongly resist attending work or family events. Often described as emotionally cold, they take pleasure in few, if any, activities, including sex. While there is some evidence for a genetic origin, some do have a history of abuse, trauma, or neglect that caused them to shut out people and emotions to protect themselves from further pain. Certainly the impact of having a parent like this would be profound. The assumption that one was not loved because of the detachment of this person would be understandable. As an adult, the best one can do to repair these feelings is to recognize that this parent was unable to love and nurture due to circumstances beyond their control and to then surround oneself with people who are capable of feeling and expressing love.

Antisocial Personality Disorder

Antisocial Personality Disorder is the clinical definition of what we usually refer to as a sociopath. This is a person who exhibits total disregard for the feelings and rights of others. They fail to conform to the social and legal norms of society and have no compunction about violating the law, which they do repeatedly. They lie at will, feel contempt for others, whom they view as stupid or gullible, and experience no remorse over taking advantage of or harming others. They are irritable, easily offended, impulsive, often violent, and indifferent to consequences. They are highly irresponsible, often moving from job to job due to inconsistent work behavior and failure to honor obligations. They are dangerous and will not hesitate to do whatever it takes to get what they want. While this diagnosis tends to run in families, this may be due more to environmental factors than genetic ones. Children of APD parents will often grow up fearful and conflict-avoidant or have significant anger issues.

While this is not a complete list of personality disorders, it does cover the disorders most likely to have caused difficulties for offspring and to catch them off guard in adulthood, creating problems for clergy who encounter these disorders in their congregants. If you have recognized a parent or other family member within these descriptions, see if you can identify people in your current life who are stirring up difficult feelings for you. Do they exhibit similar traits to a family member with a personality disorder, thereby creating an exaggerated reaction in you? Processing these insights and emotions with a therapist or trusted friend is a good way to bring about healing and the awareness of how you respond to congregants who trigger strong emotional reactions in you. Armed with insight, you can begin to develop healthier ways of responding in order to create good boundaries and improve your functioning in the church. If you want to learn more about personality disorders, there are some excellent books listed in the appendix.

Loss

Loss is a part of life and is not limited to the death of a loved one. Grief and loss can also be experienced due to a divorce or loss of other significant relationships, loss of a true childhood due to abuse or neglect, and loss of health due to injury or illness. Some people may also experience feelings

22

of grief when a door closes on their dreams—for example, a young athlete who dreams of a career in professional sports then suffers a severe injury that eliminates the possibility of pursuing their dream.

In addition to the personal losses that clergy suffer, such as the death of a loved one, et cetera, there are also a number of losses that are particular to the profession. For those whose denominations routinely move them to different churches every few years, clergy and their families are impacted by the loss of a familiar worshipping community and the caring relationships made there. In addition, clergy deal with loss on a regular basis as they walk with a congregation through deaths, tragedies, and debilitating illnesses. Pastors of aging congregations may find themselves officiating at more and more funerals and memorial services than in years past. Over time, the emotional strain of being an integral part of the dying and death of numerous church members can be overwhelming.

My sister, who is now a retired Presbyterian pastor, had a string of twelve deaths in her congregation during one year of her ministry. This also happened to be the same year that our father died. In fact, the phone call to inform her of his passing came while she was performing yet another funeral. Needless to say, the cumulative effect of all these losses seriously impacted the way she experienced her grief over our father's death.

Over the years, I have noticed that too often clergy are so focused on providing pastoral care to the families and their congregations during times of loss, they fail to acknowledge their own grief. The intensity of walking with the dying congregant and their family is such that close relationships form, and often there is no time in the aftermath to process the pastor's own feelings of loss over the person who has died. Tasks that have been ignored due to hospital visits and funeral arrangements claim the pastor's time and other urgent matters come to the fore, filling up any space that might be used to do the work of grieving.

Ultimately, grief that is not recognized has a tendency to pile up at a subconscious level. Grief that is not actively attended to can creep up on you when you least expect it, catching you off guard and leading to emotional breakdowns, sometimes in public situations where keeping one's composure is critical. Another pastor that I worked with learned of the death of a high-school classmate too late to be able to attend the memorial service. This classmate was a woman that he had been close friends with but hadn't seen in several years. The news came during a time when he had also lost a number of elderly congregants as well as an aging parent. This death of a friend put his grief quotient way over the top, and he became overwhelmed by this loss. During that time, he was emotionally fragile, crying easily and often, sometimes from the pulpit. He preached about it for several weeks, unable to move on from his deep sorrow. As we processed the intensity of his grief, it became clear that the cumulative effect of previous losses that had not been sufficiently grieved had turned this one death into the proverbial straw that broke the camel's back.

While this type of situation is one factor in how we handle grief, it is also important to recognize that early family-of-origin messages about grief play a critical role in our personal responses to loss. A close friend and colleague of mine lost her beloved grandfather when she was ten years old. At the graveside service following the funeral, her father noticed her weeping. He grabbed her arm to yank her aside, and said, "Don't ever let me see you crying about this again!" Needless to say, this greatly impacted how she dealt with grief from that point forward. Even though she continued to shed tears when such losses came along, she would beat herself up for being such a baby and repeat those internalized messages from her father, leading to undue shame and embarrassment.

I'm sure my father wasn't the only stoic to emerge from the Depression and World War II years, so it's likely that many of us learned that loss is to be met with a stiff upper lip and a "carry on" attitude. Once, when a close friend of my mother's passed away, I called to lend support to my mom on the evening after the memorial service. When my father answered the phone, I asked him how he and Mom were doing. "Oh, fine," he said breezily, "It was a nice funeral. Nobody cried." Fortunately, I was an adult at the time and capable of dismissing this absurd inference about the inappropriateness of tears at a funeral without internalizing it as a young child might do.

Many of my therapy clients who had lost loved ones in childhood told me that the dead family member was never talked about again. In fact, death was never discussed at all, and their parents didn't express grief, shed tears in the children's presence, or talk to them about the loss or the kind of feelings they might be experiencing. No memories of the loved one were shared around the dinner table. Some felt it was as though this person had never existed at all. These are just a few of the ways in which families can influence how we might deal (or *not* deal) with death and loss.

Regardless of those messages and the time constraints of ministry, it is essential for the mental health of a pastor to learn to recognize and address grief issues when they arise. It is also important to know that most models of grief are not as helpful as theorists have led us to believe. The familiar stages of grief by Elizabeth Kubler-Ross—denial, anger, bargaining, depression, and acceptance—were actually originally written to describe the experience of people who were terminally ill. Experience has taught me that grief doesn't happen in stages or cycles. It doesn't have a linear progression that we can identify and check off our list until, at some point in the future, we will "arrive," and our grief will be over. Grief is not predictable. It is also more complex than the list of emotions that are typically enumerated in grief literature. To believe that shock, anger, depression, blame, et cetera, are the only things we're going to feel is overly simplistic. I once asked a group of people attending a workshop to name all the emotions they associated with grief, and by the time we were done, I had filled an entire white board with emotion words.

There is no one right way to "do" grief. You must give yourself permission to feel whatever you feel and call it normal. You will have good days and bad days. If you find yourself crying at the drop of a hat at a time when you would rather not, schedule yourself a time to cry when nobody's watching. Let it out. Journal your grief. Share your memories and find ways to commemorate these people who were an important part of your life. Keep a picture by your bed or on your mantel. Carry something that belonged to them in your wallet or purse. Write down some of your favorite stories or sayings of this person. Create a loving ritual that will help you say good-bye in a way that meets your needs. Receive the care and comfort of others. Hugs help. If anyone tells you that "anticipatory grief" will make the grief afterwards easier, don't believe them. If you find there are things you just can't face yet, give yourself the grace to trust your instincts. If you suspect there are losses from your past that haven't been fully resolved yet, know that it is never too late to grieve. Trust that, in time, these words of the psalmist will be true for you as well, "You have turned my mourning into dancing; you have taken off my sackcloth and clothed me with joy."[4] However, if it feels like you need professional help on this journey, seek out a competent and caring therapist or spiritual director to walk with you.

4. Ps 30:11.

Taking Time to Process and Heal

If you have recognized yourself and your family of origin in the various sections of this chapter, or if by reading it you have come to understand the depth to which a particular experience, person, or family dynamic wounded you, take some time to journal about these wounds. Name them for what they are and explore how they have impacted your life. Now that you have become more aware of your areas of deepest vulnerability to the people and situations in your life that are problematic, it's time to address them more directly. It's time to acknowledge the unhealthy coping mechanisms you adopted in childhood in order to protect yourself or diminish the pain, because while they might have worked for you then, they are probably no longer serving you well. In fact, they may be creating more problems for you than the ones you were once trying to avoid. The insights you gain through this process can be helpful to you in understanding yourself better and identifying areas that need healing and growth.

It is important to realize, however, that insight is never enough. Insight alone will not change the unhealthy behaviors that impede your ability to function in your church or in your relationships with family and friends. Only *you* can do that. Healing from childhood wounds is a process, and it takes time and courage. Go slow. Honor your feelings. Be gentle with yourself. Seek professional help if you feel like you are stuck and unable to move forward. Recognize that we all have our kryptonite. No one is immune. You cannot pretend it isn't there or that it won't affect your ability to function in ministry. It will. What matters is that you become aware of it and seek to heal from it. Remember that you don't have to travel that road alone. God will bring companions alongside you to walk with you on the path to healing.

Reflection Questions

1. Was your family enmeshed or distant? As a child, how did you perceive this?

2. Was there addiction or abuse in your family? If so, how did it impact you?

3. What family role in the twelve-step model did you identify with the most? What did that look like? What were the benefits/disadvantages

of that role? Are you continuing that role in your church or nuclear family? With what effect?

4. Did one or both of your parents exhibit symptoms of a personality disorder? Which one? How did that impact you? Did that relationship contribute to any depression, anxiety, or insecurity you experience? Do you put up barriers of distrust, detachment, or defensiveness? Have your experiences of wounding impacted your ability to maintain healthy boundaries? Are you often irritable or angry, and do you have difficulty controlling that anger?

5. Did you experience a significant loss in childhood that impacted you deeply? In what ways? What were the messages, spoken or unspoken, that prevent you from acknowledging or processing grief in healthy ways?

6. When you are engaged in conflict with a person or group that stirs up uncomfortable emotions or that you realize you are not handling well, who do they remind you of? What feelings do they evoke in you? Is it possible there is a connection to unresolved emotional wounds?

7. If you become aware of unhealthy patterns of behavior in yourself, or if you repeatedly find yourself mired down in the same types of situations over and over, how might this pattern be a replication of the dynamics in your family of origin?

8. As an adult, what are the resources, both internal and external, that are available to you now that were not present in childhood? How can you use those resources to heal and to learn better ways of coping?

9. How can you distinguish between the people who were the source of your wounds and the person who may be pushing your buttons in the present?

In the next chapter, I will explore a few of the most frequent personal issues that arise from the wounds we have discussed in this chapter.

4

Kryptonite II

The Aftermath of Wounding

My grace is sufficient for you, for power is made perfect in weakness.

—I Corinthians 12:9

Guilt and Shame

Even in what some people would consider normal families, there are messages or events that can create guilt and shame that we carry with us into adulthood. Normal is not necessarily healthy. Parents, siblings, teachers, and other adults in our lives can purposefully or unintentionally cause us to experience shame and self-blame. Frequent criticism in childhood can lead to low self-esteem and the tendency to question oneself or to regularly take the blame for negative outcomes. Adults who are well-intentioned can also instill shame as they seek to correct inappropriate behaviors and teach skills that will serve us well into adulthood.

One of the factors that plays into this dynamic is the egocentric thinking of childhood. Another name for this is magical thinking. Prior to adolescence, children are not yet capable of discerning cause and effect objectively. They believe that everything that happens is somehow connected to them. They are their only point of reference. Therefore, many children tend to think they are to blame for the things that go wrong in their lives. A good example of this comes from the 1990's sitcom *Wings*. Two brothers, Joe and Brian, owned a small airfield, which they ran together. Sadly, they had experienced abandonment by their mother at a young age, and Brian, the younger of the two, had been quite traumatized by this event. When their mother came to see them at the airfield many years later, it came out that Brian had broken his mother's favorite vase the night before she left. For all those years of her absence from their lives, he had believed that she left because she was so angry over the broken vase. Even though this incident was not connected in any way to her leaving, Brian had continued to blame himself. He was too young to have been aware of the marital difficulties that were the true reason for her absence from his life.

Another contributor to feelings of guilt is the teachings of rigid and judgmental church communities. Many people grew up listening to fire-and-brimstone preachers and Sunday school teachers that focused more on the rules of the Bible than on the good news of God's unconditional love. These churches are not limited to conservative or evangelical denominations. Marcus Borg, one of the great progressive Christian writers, was raised in the Lutheran church and remembers that for a long time he was more focused on avoiding hell than he was on being in relationship with a God of hope and love.[1] When we hear this kind of routine condemnation of "bad behavior" and violation of the rules, it is easy to develop a tendency toward guilt and fear of punishment. When things go awry in our world, the fallback position is that it must have been our fault.

In adulthood, those who suffer from guilt and self-blame often take responsibility for negative outcomes far beyond what is warranted. If anything goes wrong in their family or in the church, they believe that it is their own fault, and they alone are responsible for fixing the problem. One of the ways I use to help people challenge their beliefs about this is to have them create a "responsibility pie." I ask them to draw a circle on a piece of paper, then to the side of it write the names of the other people involved in the situation. Then I ask them to ascribe an appropriate percentage of responsibility to each of those people and draw it in on the pie chart. It doesn't take long for them to see that they were not the only one who contributed to the situation, and often, by the time they add in the wedges of everyone else, there's very little of the pie left for them to fill in their own name.

The trouble with excessive guilt is that we often build an altar to it. We visit that altar on a regular basis to rend our clothes and lift up burnt offerings when a simple and honest repentance would suffice. Dwelling on our mistakes is a lot like driving down the highway while looking in

1. Borg, *Convictions*, 29–30.

the rear-view mirror. You can't see where you're going, and you're likely to get in a wreck. It's much better to acknowledge what was truly your part, consider how you might better handle a similar situation in the future, and then move on.

So what is the difference between guilt and shame? The most widely recognized definition is that guilt is experienced over something one has done, and shame is experienced for who you are. Most often, shame occurs as a result of parental neglect or emotional, physical, and/or sexual abuse. When abuse and neglect occur without a clear connection to a behavior, children tend to believe they must be innately bad or unworthy of love for this kind of treatment to occur. Victims of abuse are often given messages such as:

"You make me do this!"

"I wish you'd never been born."

"You make me want to run away."

"Leave me alone. I can't be bothered with you right now."

"You disgust me!"

Given the prevalence of dysfunctional families of origin among clergy, it stands to reason that this kind of abuse may have been present in many clergy's lives. If this is the origin of one's feelings of shame, it is vital for the abuse to be addressed through a therapeutic process with a qualified mental health professional. In addition, a spiritual journey of discovering one's worth in the sight of God can help to heal these wounds. Knowing that you are beloved by God just as you are, that you are chosen and blessed, and that the abuse was not your fault is a balm for the wounded spirit who suffered from childhood abuse of any kind. Repeating positive self-affirmations or writing them in your journal can also help in overcoming the shadow of shame. In addition, there are a number of excellent books on this topic that are listed in the appendix at the end of this book.

Fear and Anxiety

As we explored in the previous chapter, children who were raised in unsafe environments or with anxious and overprotective parents can grow up to be fearful and anxious adults. New situations or environments can be anxiety-producing and sometimes even overwhelming. Fears can run rampant, and anxious thoughts can fill your head with "what ifs." Like a child who fears monsters under the bed at night, imaginary dangers may seem to lurk around every corner. Free-floating anxiety can pervade your thoughts and hamper your ability to focus and function. People with a history of abuse are particularly prone to something called hypervigilance, in which one is constantly on the lookout for danger, scanning one's surroundings for potential hazards or unsafe people or situations. Perfectionism is another form of anxiety in which one is constantly seeking to measure up to some impossible standard of excellence that will confirm one's worthiness. All of these can have the consequence of preventing clergy from functioning effectively and confidently in their churches, families, and community.

A certain amount of fear is normal. When we face new situations in which we don't know what to expect, it is natural to have some fear and anxiety. Despite this, most people are able to move past their fears and embrace the new circumstances or experiences in which they find themselves. But when fear prevents one from doing things that would be rewarding, fun, or necessary in order to accomplish a goal, then the fear is unhealthy and counterproductive. If you notice that your fears are holding you back from living the life you want, then it is time to address them directly and face the monster. A former adviser of mine had a favorite saying that, "If you can name it, you can tame it." In other words, naming your fears is half the battle. Ask yourself what you are afraid of. Get it out into the open where you can look at it and see it for what it really is. In the book, *Feel the Fear and Do It Anyway*, author Susan Jeffers posits that every fear basically comes down to the idea that, whatever it is, we can't handle it. When we face our fears, they feel a little less scary. We can confront the belief that we would be unable to handle the eventualities that we fear. If you look at them with a clear mind, you may realize that you probably *could* handle it. It might be uncomfortable or painful, but you do possess the skills to deal with the negative events that you imagine. And if you don't, you can go about cultivating those skills, whether they be self-defense, resilience, courage, or the ability to remain calm in a crisis. You can plan a course of action for the possible scenarios you invent in your head.

A similar strategy is helpful for the anxious thoughts that clutter up our mind and keep us from functioning at peak capacity. In the field of cognitive behavioral therapy, it is understood that our emotions are primarily driven by our thoughts about an event or interaction. The problem comes when the thought about an experience is irrational. For example, you may walk into the church one morning, and instead of the usual cheery greeting from your administrative assistant, you are met with stony silence. People who tend to take things personally might automatically think, "What did I do wrong?" which then leads to anxiety, anger, or defensiveness. However, this is likely an irrational belief; the assistant's mood might just as easily be the result of a bad night's sleep or an argument with his or her spouse. Confronting the irrational thought can help to prevent the emotional upset that might follow if the thought went unchallenged. Replacing such cognitive distortions with a more realistic perspective makes all the difference.

The irrational thought exemplified in the previous example is called personalization. Another typical cognitive distortion is catastrophizing, sometimes referred to as "awfulizing."[2] This is what we do when we anticipate negative events and exaggerate just how awful they are going to be when they do occur. We anticipate the worst-case scenario. This intensifies our anxiety exponentially. One time I was speaking to a group of college students about the cognitive distortions we are discussing here and I asked them to give me an example of something they were afraid of. One young man raised his hand and said, "I'm afraid of failing my physics final." The other students chuckled sympathetically. I asked him what he thought would happen if he did, and without hesitation, he responded, "My parents will kick me out." When I asked him if he really thought that was true, he had to acknowledge that they probably wouldn't react that drastically, but would nonetheless be displeased. We agreed that being displeased was much easier to deal with than being kicked out of the house, which allowed him to face his final exam with less anxiety and probably resulted in a higher score as a consequence.

Another major contributor to anxiety is the belief in an external locus of control. In this cognitive distortion, people believe that they have no control over events and are helpless victims of fate. Things are perceived as happening *to* them, rather than them having agency over their own lives. When someone holds this belief, it is easy to see how he or she might be anxious about potential negative events. It creates a sense of helplessness that makes every day seem fraught with peril.

Of course, we are all familiar with the demon of "shoulds." This thought pattern is often at the center of those with perfectionistic tendencies and thus performance anxiety. We are all weighed down with a big bag of shoulds that we collected from our families, our teachers, our churches,

2. For a thorough list of cognitive distortions, see Appendix A.

et cetera. The problem is that we internalize them in childhood and then never challenge them later in life. We never look at those shoulds and evaluate them to see if they really fit with our adult values and beliefs. Instead, we use them as weapons to beat ourselves up with on a regular basis. A complicating factor is that we tend to rebel against rules, which makes it harder to follow them, providing even more opportunities to fail at living up to the shoulds. The best way to combat this is to start being more aware of self-talk that is laden with the words "should," "must," or "have to." When you catch yourself doing it, stop for a moment, pull that should out of the bag, and look at it with some discernment. Ask yourself if this is something you truly believe, if it is in keeping with your sense of what is important in life. Is it of value, or is it something you can let go of? Is it realistic, or impossible to live up to? Is it a belief or value that is life-enhancing or life-restricting? Is it rigid, or can it be applied more flexibly, depending on circumstances? Once you answer these questions, you can decide whether to set that should aside or claim it as a value that you now take as your own. The interesting thing is that when you do that, it has now become a *choice* as opposed to a should. That allows you to change your language around this value, which changes how you react to it. It allows you to be more gentle with yourself, which in turn reduces your anxiety and fear around failing to live up to impossible expectations.

One caveat—if your fear and anxiety are a part of a cluster of symptoms arising from post-traumatic stress disorder due to childhood trauma or other traumatic events, it is of vital importance that you seek professional help to address those issues. These few paragraphs will not be sufficient to help you deal with the sometimes overpowering symptoms of physical, emotional, or sexual abuse.

Anger

Anger is such a problematic emotion, especially in the church. Scriptural texts in both the Old and New Testament seem to indicate that anger is a bad thing that needs to be avoided at all costs. In Proverbs, only fools give vent to their anger while the wise hold their tongues. In Matthew, Jesus says, "But I say to you that if you are angry with a brother or sister, you will be liable to judgment."[3] Even James chimes in on the subject when he

3. Matt 5:22a.

admonishes, "Your anger does not produce God's righteousness."[4] Most of us know it's impossible to eliminate anger from our lives, yet we are left feeling guilty when anger does rear its head. Family messages about anger also contribute to our angst about feeling or expressing anger. As children, many of us were taught that anger is not okay and were the recipient of strict punishment for angry outbursts. This was especially confusing if we witnessed the frequent anger of our parents. To a small child, seeing a grown-up expressing anger in frightening ways can be overwhelming. As an adult, we never want to emulate that behavior, and this may lead to repression of angry feelings and thoughts. The trouble is that anger doesn't just go away. Like magma building up under a volcano, anger is going to find a way out, and the more one holds it in, the more explosive it will be when it ultimately erupts.

One of the barriers to a healthier attitude towards anger is the common belief that anger and aggression are the same thing. Anger is an emotion; aggression is a behavior. While aggression might be one person's way of dealing with their anger, it doesn't have to be your way. While we often categorize emotions as either bad or good, they are actually value neutral. They are a natural part of our response to life in all its permutations. Think of emotions as a rainbow. The full spectrum of human emotion is a gift from God, and if we are created in the image of God, then every emotion we have is in God and of God. If one were to remove one color from the rainbow, it would no longer be complete. The fullness of a healthy emotional life will occasionally include anger. So, if God can get angry, why can't we?

A cursory survey of scriptures related to God's anger highlights some differences between the qualities of God's anger versus human anger. Numerous psalms speak of a God who is slow to anger, while humans are often quick-tempered and easily roused to anger. God's anger in the Hebrew Bible is most often aimed at injustice, and we see this also in the person of Jesus, who railed against injustice and hypocrisy, as exemplified by the overturning of the money changers' tables in the temple[5] or his rant against the Pharisees in the "Seven Woes" passage.[6] Thus, righteous anger can be viewed in a positive light as God's people respond to suffering and injustice in the world. God is also quick to forgive, yet we often hold on to grudges and resentments long past their expiration date. It also

4. Jas 1:20.
5. Matt 21:12.
6. Matt 23.

34

seems that God's anger arises out of God's love for us and a desire to be in covenant relationship. Instead, human anger tends to arise out of ego, unmet expectations, jealousy, fear, and the need for control. God's anger usually results in thoughtful and loving discipline, while humanity reacts impulsively, sometimes responding to perceived slights with vengeful or hurtful actions. This comparison can help us more accurately assess our own anger and begin a process of becoming more God-like in the way we experience and respond to anger.

With so many messages about the "evils" of anger, can we find anything positive about it? I believe that anger is actually essential to our healing from emotional wounds. Anger can be a source of the determination and strength of will needed to propel you onto the path of healing. Anger can serve as an alarm system that tells you that something is wrong in your world and energizes you to take action to correct the situation. Anger can be self-honoring, especially for victims of abuse. It speaks to the reality that they didn't deserve the abuse; indeed what they deserved instead was love, respect, and safety. Anger can serve as a catalyst for change in oneself, one's relationships, or in society as a whole. This is at the heart of Jesus' passion for social justice. A current example is the founder of Mothers Against Drunk Drivers (MADD). In the early 1980s, Candy Lightner lost her teenage daughter in a drunk-driving accident. It was her anger at this needless death that propelled her to form the organization that has been instrumental in the huge reduction in drunk-driving deaths over the past thirty-five years. There are many, many other examples of people who used their anger as a starting point for growth and healing, the repair of a relationship, or to bring about positive change in the community or in the larger culture.

Now for the downside of anger—when anger is held onto, when it becomes the primary focus of your thoughts and actions, it can become toxic. Long-term resentment and hostility are incredibly damaging to your physical, emotional, and social well-being. The Buddha is often cited as the originator of the maxim, "Resentment is like drinking poison and waiting for the other person to die." Holding on to resentment doesn't harm the recipient of your anger at all, but it can greatly damage you! Toxic anger can result in obsessive thoughts, sleepless nights, and physical symptoms such as hypertension, indigestion, and a compromised immune system. It also greatly limits your capacity for joy and your ability to feel peace in the presence of God.

When you become aware that your anger is a problem in your life, it's time to do something about it. You can begin by noticing your thoughts about the situation that is making you angry. Watch for cognitive distortions or irrational thoughts, such as "shoulds" (this time about how other people *should* behave), black and white thinking, the fallacy that life is fair, personalization, or labeling. (See Appendix A.) Remember that other people don't always ascribe to the same values as you. While that would be your preference, it isn't realistic to expect that others will naturally fall in line with your preferred way of being and relating. There is a theory that 90 percent of anger is unmet expectations. So whether you are dealing with the church secretary who failed to accomplish something you had asked her or him to do or the person who continually critiques your sermon, it is a perfectly normal human reaction to get angry. The challenge is to develop the ability to let it go, so it doesn't eat away at you and turn into ongoing hostility. See if you can unpack the expectations you have for this person and ask yourself if they are realistic. Also, be aware that the person you're angry with might have other things going on in their life that are impacting how they feel and act. It's not always about you. Consider the possibility that you have labeled this person to the extent that they have become one-dimensional for you, that you are seeing them through the lens of your own bias. Looking at them as a whole person with many aspects can help you see their positive traits as well as their flaws. Journaling can be helpful in this process, as can talking the situation through with a spouse, colleague, or trusted advisor.

More than most other emotions, anger is often quite visceral. You feel it in your body, in your muscles, and in your gut. There are times when you need a physical release for your anger. That's when it is helpful to go outside and dig in the dirt if you enjoy gardening, or go running or work out at the gym. And when you really just need to throw something, take a container of ice cubes into your bathroom and throw them one at a time against your shower wall. They will shatter satisfyingly and fall into the tub where they will melt and disappear. No muss, no fuss, nothing valuable broken in the process! As the ice melts, realize that it is possible to just let it go.

Forgiveness

Preaching on forgiveness or engaging in theological discussions about forgiveness is far different from actually practicing it in the areas of deepest wounding in your own life. Forgiveness is *hard*! And yet, forgiveness is also a path of release from the difficult memories of the past. I believe it is a mistake to think that forgiveness is primarily for the benefit of the person who sinned against you. Instead, forgiveness is the act that sets the one who was wronged free from their victimhood and allows them to put the past behind them, thus creating a new future without being controlled by the memories and wounds of yesterday.

I believe that forgiveness is more of a process than a single act of absolution. Instead, it is a gradual letting go that takes time and intention. Matthew, Sheila, and Dennis Linn, authors of the book *Don't Forgive Too Soon,* posit that the process of forgiveness can mirror the stages of grief set out by Elizabeth Kubler-Ross, and in this case, the stages are quite helpful. Another excellent book about forgiveness is *Forgiveness, the Passionate Journey* by Flora Slosson Wuellner. She offers a nine-step journey to forgiveness with the Beatitudes as guide. Both of these books help to dispel the "once and done" attitude that creates resistance and guilt for a person who has been deeply harmed by another. This belief can cause someone to forgive too soon, short-circuiting the healing process. According to Margaret Guenther, "the wound of abuse is like any other deep and infected wound. If the surface is allowed to heal over too quickly, poison remains to spread sickness deep within."[7]

When we realize that forgiveness is a process, it allows us to be more gentle with ourselves. We don't have to feel guilty or allow others to shame us for failing to forgive on a prescribed timeline. We can't forgive before we're ready. Ignatius of Loyola, in his Spiritual Exercises, offers a more gradual practice of forgiveness. He suggests that if you find yourself unable to forgive, ask God for the desire to forgive. And if even that is too much, ask God for the desire to desire to forgive. This gives necessary distance and breathing room from which to contemplate what forgiveness is and what it is not.

We have many misconceptions about what forgiveness means that put barriers in the way of our ability to consider that forgiveness is possible. Lewis Smedes addresses this in his classic book, *Forgive and Forget.* That old adage that forgiving means forgetting is the first fallacy that has to go! It suggests that to forgive means that we must also forget the hurts we've suffered entirely. For one thing, it's just not possible. In physiological terms, the brain's filtering process of what we remember and what we forget is mostly out of our control. We cannot just decide to forget something. And

7. Guenther, *Holy Listening,* 138.

the memories our brains retain cannot and often *should not* be forgotten. To forget an event that caused us harm could leave us open to further victimization in the future. To forget would prevent us from recognizing potentially harmful situations and thus acting in ways that protect us.

Forgiveness also does not mean that we put ourselves in a position to be hurt again by the one who harmed us in the past. We do not have to be a doormat for their bad treatment. At this point, some readers might want to point out Jesus' admonition to "turn the other cheek."[8] However, if you look at this passage from the context of ancient Hebrew culture, it is clear that Jesus didn't actually mean we should stay in situations where we can too easily be hurt again and again. In actuality, Jesus was talking about passive resistance to oppression. In that hierarchical society, masters struck their servants back-handed. This was easily accomplished with the right hand. However, if the servant turned his other cheek for another blow, the master would be forced to use his left hand, which was unclean, or strike him with his right fist, which would indicate equality with the servant. Thus, the likelihood would be that the master would just walk away rather than violate the dictates of either "church" or society.[9]

Forgiveness does not require reconciliation. Just because someone has reached a point in their healing process where forgiveness is possible, doesn't mean he or she needs to be in relationship with the person who wronged them. In fact, severing ties with this person might be the only way one can continue to heal or to be safe. It is okay to maintain a firm boundary between yourself and the other.

Another thing forgiveness is not is excusing someone for what they did. According to Joseph Driskill, "Forgiveness goes hand in hand with justice."[10] Even when forgiveness is given, those who have wronged you may still be held accountable in whatever way is appropriate. Your forgiveness is not a message that what they did was okay.

Finally, I believe that forgiveness is not a spectator sport. It is a private affair, something between you and the offender, and sometimes just between you and God. It is nobody else's business. Far too many people feel free to weigh in on whether you should or shouldn't forgive, whether you're taking too long, or exactly how you should communicate that forgiveness. In order to avoid the judgment of others, I have known individuals who have publicly

8. Matt 5:39.
9. Linn et al., *Don't Forgive Too Soon*, 5.
10. See Driskill, "Traumatized Persons," 32.

forgiven someone, yet continued to hold on to the hurt and pain for years, prematurely cutting off the forgiveness process because they just hadn't been ready yet. And that's okay, too. We're human. We forgive slowly, piece by piece, layer by layer, over and over again. Perhaps that's what Jesus meant when he told us we needed to forgive seventy-seven times![11] He knew that in our humanness, it would take that many times to get it right.

Some Thoughts on Suffering

Often when we're hurting, we get bogged down in the *why* of suffering. We wonder what we did to deserve the painful things in our lives. We look for an explanation that will somehow make us feel better, that will make sense out of something that seems senseless. Or we look for someone to blame. Knowing why something happened makes us feel as though we have the ability to prevent bad things from happening to us. It allows us to imagine that we are in control. We think that if we know the answer to the why of our hurts, it will somehow make a difference. But what it won't do is help us work through the process of healing. True healing is about moving beyond the why and seeking to make meaning of our suffering.

Making meaning is the act of looking for the gift that somehow re-deems your suffering or helps you to transcend your pain. For clergy, it is often their own troubles that have broken them open to the pain of the world. For some, brokenness can be the crucible for a deep compassion that enables them to walk with the members of their congregations through some of the most difficult circumstances one can imagine. Henri Nouwen puts it this way, "[Our] painful times have proven to be the times that made us able to give more instead of less. Our brokenness opens us to a deeper way of sharing our lives and offering each other hope. Just as bread needs to be broken in order to be given, so, too, do our lives."[12]

This is a common theme among people who have suffered deep emo-tional wounds. Often, toward the end of a process of therapy with someone, I will ask them "What are the positive things about you and your current life that are a direct consequence of your suffering?" One of my long-term clients, a woman with a profound history of sexual abuse, once responded after much thought, "Well, I have this big old heart!" And she did. Others have named special people that came into their lives during times of their

11. Matt 18:22.
12. Nouwen, *Life of the Beloved*, 88.

deepest pain. Some have identified the hurtful incident as a turning point in their life or career that took them down a different path, one that led to wholeness and joy. Some people name qualities such as wisdom, compassion, or the ability to see past the trivialities of life and recognize what is truly important. They also seem to be able to live more in the moment, knowing that nothing in life is guaranteed.

One of the discoveries that comes up time and time again is the realization that God is a creative God who uses even the most painful experiences to shape us and use us. God does not waste anything, and God has the power to transform suffering beyond our wildest imaginings. I urge you to enter into your own process of discovery, considering the ways that God has used even your darkest times to shape you into who you are today. Can you view that as gift? This does not mean you are glad for the bad things that happened, but that you are grateful for God's transforming power that is made evident in the way you have been healed and then offered yourself, like loaves and fishes, for the good of the world.

Reflection Questions

1. What is the source of guilt and shame in your life? What messages did you receive, spoken or unspoken, about who you are as a person? Can you examine those messages, challenge their meaning, and offer yourself grace?

2. What are your fears? Do they prevent you from living life to the fullest? What can you do to reduce their power over you?

3. What makes you most angry? Can you identify the consequences of holding on to your anger? What gets in the way of letting go of built-up anger and resentment?

4. Who or what do you feel you need to forgive? What is making that difficult to do? What is one step you can take that will put you on the path to forgiveness, keeping in mind that forgiveness is a journey, not a singular event.

5. What is your theology of suffering? Does that help or hinder your ability to heal from your deepest wounds? Can you identify the gift that arose out of your suffering? If you are struggling in this area, consider seeking the help of a spiritual director who can walk with you during this journey.

5

Boundaries, Expectations, and Other Demons

At the time, discipline isn't much fun. It always feels like it's going against the grain. Later, of course, it pays off handsomely, for it's the well-trained who find themselves mature in their relationship with God.

—HEBREWS 12:11 (THE MESSAGE)

Boundaries

In the United Methodist Church, as in many mainline denominations, clergy are required to receive eight hours of boundary training every four years. Whenever a reminder to sign up for these workshops is given, a collective groan goes up. Nobody really likes to attend these day-long classes that cover the same ground time after time. Pastors feel that the training is just one long lecture on what not to do. They know what the rules are, but they fight what feels like rigid strictures that sometimes get in the way of caring ministry. Often, the larger church emphasizes the importance of protecting parishioners from over-zealous pastors and inappropriate relationships, but that is not the whole picture. What clergy need to realize is that boundaries are also crucial in protecting pastors from church members whose inability to tolerate boundaries causes them to

41

continually encroach on your time, attention, and even space. Ultimately, healthy personal boundaries are the essential ingredient for the ability of clergy to create the time and space necessary for good self-care, including the facets of physical, spiritual, vocational, and relational health that make up the remainder of this book.

Parishioners are infamous for not respecting boundaries. They want their pastor to be at their beck and call, they want you to be their best friend and share deeply personal information with them, or they walk into the parsonage without knocking, because it's owned by the church, as if that somehow gives them the right. Congregants continually blur the line between your public and private life. If you don't set clear boundaries with them, nobody else will. Your position as the pastor of your church puts you in a position of power, and it is up to you to set the standard for consistent and healthy boundaries. You need to be overt in setting guidelines around your time, space, relationships, and selfhood.

But what exactly are boundaries anyway? They are the dividing lines between what belongs to me and what belongs to you. They are the markers of what is me versus what is not me. They are a way of defining space. In that way, our skin is a boundary, just like the fence between your house and your neighbor's is a boundary. Some boundaries shift, like the boundary where sea meets shore, and some are more rigid, like the Great Wall of China. Some are permeable, like a picket fence, others are impermeable, like a cement highway barrier.

Let's use this fence metaphor as a way to explore the advantages and disadvantages of various kinds of boundaries. Let's suppose that you live on a square block of homes where there are no fences. The entire space behind the houses is a wide open grassy area where the children can play with total freedom. Of course, the kids love this freedom. It gives them a bigger space to play their games, to run, climb trees, etc. The parents might not like it so much, however, as morning after morning they wake up to find other kids' belongings in their yard and their children's things scattered all over the neighborhood. They end up having to return other people's stuff and wander the open area searching for a lost coat or ball or bicycle. Not much fun. So the parents of this neighborhood get together and solve the problem by each family agreeing to erect a five-foot cement block fence to keep everybody's stuff in their own yard. Suddenly, the kids have lost their play space and have to go out the front door and knock on their neighbor's front door in order to play together, probably in the street. They are not happy. The parents are pleased with this resolution of the problem initially, because their children aren't losing so much stuff, but over time, they miss the interaction of talking with their neighbors on a summer evening in the back yard or hosting a big neighborhood barbecue.

What is the solution? Perhaps it is that picket fence I mentioned earlier, which allows for the give and take of conversation and community, with a gate that allows children to come and go with permission, while still drawing lines about what belongs to whom. Now, there still might be neighbors who don't respect the fence and decide to use that gate to come over and walk in your back door without knocking. With people like this you will need a higher fence or a lock on the gate. This fence metaphor is a good way to visualize the need for boundaries and the types of boundaries that are necessary in a variety of situations.

When we are discussing the boundaries between people, the line is an invisible one, which makes it even more important to be clear about what belongs to you and what belongs to the other. In order to set appropriate boundaries around the self, it's helpful to understand what that includes. The graphic below gives a visual for what a fence around your self would contain. Just as your skin defines the boundaries of your physical self, this graphic defines the more intangible aspects of self. They make up a large part of who you are and what you are responsible for.

SELF

Emotions	Actions
Values and Beliefs	Consequences of Actions
Opinions	Decisions
Need/desires	Responsibilities
Expectations	Relationships

What is the implication of this list? To me, it means that you have a right to your own thoughts, emotions, and beliefs. You have a right to choose what actions you will take and then to accept the consequences of those actions. You also have the responsibility to own all of these things and communicate them in respectful and appropriate ways rather than expecting people to read your mind. Nobody has the right to intrude on your territory of self without invitation or the genuine desire to help. As an example, while it is perfectly acceptable for people to disagree with your beliefs or to engage in respectful dialogue about issues, they don't have the right to insist that you agree with them. Nor do they have the right to impose responsibilities on you that are not truly yours. And nobody has the right to tell you how you ought to feel or act in a given situation. When you get clear about what belongs to you and what doesn't, you may find yourself more able to be clear about your personal boundaries when you are challenged.

By the same token, everybody else carries around this same box, but in an infinite variety of iterations. We need to learn to recognize and honor the selfhood of the other. This is not always easy when my opinions or expectations bump up against your opinions or expectations. You do not have the right to impose your beliefs, values, or expectations on others, but a healthy exchange of ideas can facilitate growth for both parties. It's helpful to recognize that not everyone thinks or feels about things the same way you do, and that their story, one you may never know, has had a crucial impact on their selfhood. Compassion allows us to step outside of our own box on occasion and imagine what it's like to live in someone else's box. As the other person's pastor, you are responsible for respecting their box, the dividing line between them and you, and also for helping them to own their own stuff, which creates the possibility for healing. This is what it means to live in community. It's important to realize that our boxes aren't so fixed and rigid that there isn't opportunity for change and growth, and as clergy, you have the privilege of being a catalyst for the transformation of the people you serve.

Being clear about these aspects of self and recognizing the dividing line between yourself and the other can guide your responses when faced with criticism and/or inappropriate requests from members of your congregation. It will also prevent the criticism from chipping away at you. Here are some examples:

Example 1:

Parishioner: "Pastor Jones always did this. Why don't you?"

Response: "We all have different ways of doing things, and different people have different needs. What was important to you about how Pastor Jones did it?" (Respects the speaker's wishes without the pastor taking responsibility for it.)

Example 2:

> **Parishioner:** "I take issue with your stance on having the flag displayed in the chancel. You have no respect for our country!"
>
> **Response:** "My feelings about our country are not at issue here. What I *do* believe is that when we are in the sanctuary, we are citizens of God's kingdom above all." (Sets a boundary on the speaker presuming to know what the pastor does or doesn't believe.)

Example 3:

> **Parishioner:** "I really think you should consider letting the youth pastor go. He is putting crazy ideas in the kids' heads, and the parents are starting to complain."
>
> **Response:** "Thank you for your input. I see that you really care about our youth, but it's up to those parents to come to me with their concerns." (Refuses to allow the parishioner to dictate the pastor's actions.)

Something that's often helpful when serving a church is to set personal policies about the things you are or are not willing to do. This might include office hours, visitations, emergency phone calls, access to the parsonage, etc. It's amazing how people are often more comfortable with "policy" than a flat-out "no." Policy takes away the sting of being told "no" to their unreasonable requests. They don't have to take your refusal personally. Of course, all policies have exceptions, and you will have to discern when it is important to make an exception and when it is not.

This is particularly true when it comes to emergencies. It's not enough to tell people not to call you unless it's an emergency. You must define the nature of what you consider to be an emergency, because it's likely that it will be different than theirs. When I was a mom with young kids, and I needed some "me" time, I told them not to disturb me unless there was blood or structural damage. While this was said facetiously, it is not far from the truth. Your guidelines in the church will probably include other criteria, but it helps to have an explicit picture of what counts as an emergency and then communicate this clearly to your congregation. Nevertheless, there will be emergencies you never imagined, and the ability to have permeable boundaries will serve you well. Case in point, I was leading a clergy retreat several years ago when one of the pastors received a phone call informing her that the building which housed the church's clothing bank had burned down—not something the pastor would ever have thought to include in her list of legitimate emergencies, but it certainly met the criteria for "structural damage." She left the retreat and went home to deal with the crisis.

It's also perfectly acceptable to put some of the burden on church authorities as the source of boundaries. For example, when I was sent into a church to serve as an interim lay pastor during a time of upheaval, I wanted to get the perspective of an elderly member who had a long history with that church. I asked if he would meet me at a coffee shop, but his response was to invite me into his home for tea. Knowing I needed to establish a boundary but not wanting to offend, I told him, "Thank you so much for the invitation, but the conference, in order to avoid the appearance of impropriety, is encouraging pastors not to meet with parishioners in their homes unless another person is present." After all, Jesus did send out his disciples "two by two." The more you can refer people to the rules or recommendations of a district superintendent, moderator of presbytery, direct supervisor, or regional governing body of your church in regard to boundaries, the better.

One final note about boundaries: be especially aware of the personality disordered folks in your midst. This may require a review of the material in chapter 3 as well as the reading of one of the many excellent books about personality disorders that are on the market (see Appendix D). People with personality disorders are particularly bad at having and/or respecting boundaries. This means that you will need to be even more clear with them, which may include frequent repetitions of the boundaries you have set.

Expectations

Many new pastors stumble across the demon of a church's expectations. Some individuals and/or entire congregations may have expectations that are neither reasonable, realistic, appropriate, nor healthy, and just because a former pastor met those expectations doesn't mean it was any of those things. Often, the most troublesome are the unspoken expectations. While some of these are impossible to know until you are in the thick of a conflict or misunderstanding, the more information you have ahead of time, the better prepared you are to deal with them when they arise. Forewarned is forearmed. Speaking with the former pastor of a church to which you are newly called or appointed is a good way to gather information that will help you step with care through the minefield of expectations. Ask him or her about the traditions and expectations—spoken and unspoken—they discovered as they journeyed with this congregation. You might even include the clergyperson's spouse or life partner in this conversation if they are willing. (It's also important to hold this information loosely, as the previous pastor's experience with certain people in the church may be unfairly biased due to their own issues.)

It is also helpful to have a comprehensive meeting with the staff-parish committee about both contractual obligations and the expectations that are less clearly defined. Then meet individually with other key members of the church, such as staff people, lay leaders, and chairpersons of the administrative board, session, or vestry. These are people who can fill out the picture of what this congregation is like. You will want to know what the dynamics are, who the movers and shakers are, and who the people are that ascribe to the axiom, "It's easier to ask forgiveness than permission." Find out if there is a matriarch that wields power even though she has no official position in the church.

When you do your "due diligence" ahead of time, there will likely be fewer land mines for you to step on as you seek to lead your church. However, when the surprises do come, use those as opportunities to clarify your roles and the roles of others involved. Sometimes we don't know where boundaries need to be until there's a problem. Mistakes will be made. Learn, grow, and move on. However, if you are unable to resolve an issue on your own, don't hesitate to lean on your supervisor as an important ally. There will be times when an intermediary will be necessary for the healthy resolution of difficult situations. It is also important to remember that not every conflict is your fault. Some congregations can be toxic no matter who the pastor is and may need intervention from the church hierarchy in order to become healthier.

Be aware of your own expectations as well, especially if you are a new pastor with stars in your eyes and high hopes for your first church. Try not to project all that you want a church to be onto this congregation. Enter into ministry with your eyes and heart open, with plenty of grace for yourself and your church and room for learning what the congregation truly needs before tackling your ideal agenda. Be an observer of people, patterns, and relationships. Ask a lot of questions. Listen deeply, and remember that not everything you hear is true. Pay attention to subtext. Make every effort to be a neutral and non-anxious presence as people come to you with difficulties and desires. Express gratitude for the information, hopes, and hurts that people share with you without committing to a course of action until you have all the information.

Triangulation

Triangulation is an unhealthy pattern which involves avoidance of conflict by channeling communication through a third person. This kind of indirect communication is a normal part of childhood development, but by adulthood we should be mature enough to deal with difficult matters head on. This style of communication is often used by people who are shy, reluctant to hurt people's feelings, fearful of confrontation, manipulative, or passive-aggressive. Whatever the reason, this pattern is seldom effective and often causes more problems and hurt feelings in the long run. As is exhibited by the childhood game of Telephone where messages are passed down a line by whispering in the next person's ear, this type of communication is almost always inaccurate and lacking in essential information that would facilitate understanding.

Nonetheless, triangulation happens in churches on a regular basis. Complaints are registered with the pastor by a third party frequently, often accompanied by a refusal to reveal the complainant's name. Or someone might come to the pastor about an issue they are having with another parishioner. These people are attempting to put the pastor in the role of go-between. All of these ploys need to be stopped and redirected to other, healthier ways of communicating and resolving conflict or hurt feelings. Direct communication should be promoted as the foundation of a healthy congregation at all times. Now, this does not mean that someone who is highly introverted, has difficulty with conflict, or is from a culture where direct confrontation is not viewed as respectful couldn't bring a friend or family member with them when they come to speak to you. This would be both acceptable and gracious on the pastor's part.

In Matthew 18, Jesus gives us a guideline for communication in the church that rivals all the prevailing psychological wisdom about handling conflict. His first recommendation is, "If another member of the church sins against you, go and point out the fault when the two of you are alone. If the member listens to you, you have regained that one."[1] What this means for pastors is that if one of your congregants comes to you with a complaint about another person, you will need to tell them that it is their responsibility

1. Matt 18:15.

to work that out with the person who offended or hurt them. You can help them figure out what to say or how to approach the person, but that needs to be the extent of your involvement. The exception to this boundary is when sexual abuse has been reported. In that case, the safety of the victim is of primary concern, and a pastor should NEVER suggest that the victim confront the abuser on their own. (Most denominations have protocols for how to proceed in such instances, and those should be followed.)

In the scenario where someone comes to your office with a complaint about you from an unnamed source, you can tell them, "I have a policy not to engage in this kind of indirect communication. If the person with the complaint will come to me, I would be glad to talk to them about it."

Jesus goes on to say "But if you are not listened to, take one or two others along with you, so that every word may be confirmed by the evidence of two or three witnesses."[2] So likewise, if the person reporting a problem with another is unsuccessful in their attempt to resolve the issue, you may agree to go with them in order to support them and/or mediate the conversation, but you still shouldn't take matters into your own hands. And if the one who has sent an intermediary to pass along their complaint still refuses to come to you directly, you can tell the third-party reporter that you would be happy to meet with both of them if the other person would feel more comfortable in that situation. Otherwise, there is nothing you can do. Think back to the "box of self" that we talked about earlier. Everyone is responsible for their communication with others. If someone takes issue with something you have done, it is their responsibility to communicate that to you. You can't read their mind, and you can't hope to resolve a situation if you can't hear the concern directly from the person who has the problem.

One good rule of thumb in many situations is to stop a moment before responding to someone who has come to you with a problem and ask yourself, "Whose problem is this?" Sometimes, the problem will legitimately be yours, and you will need to respond accordingly. But if it is not yours, the answer will help you know how to redirect that person in order to appropriately resolve the situation. It is not your job to shoulder every issue that comes before you. Clarity about boundaries will allow you to respond in healthy ways, modeling good communication patterns and refusing to fall into the triangulation trap. Slipping back into our boundary metaphor of the fence, when someone attempts to put their own trash on your side of the fence, gently and kindly place it back into their yard. Even if they don't

2. Matt 18:16.

get the hint the first time, you are still modeling respect for the fence and what it stands for. Hopefully, your church will eventually get the message (although there are no guarantees).

Codependency

One of the especially tempting demons of the ministry is codependency. While codependence is a term most often used in reference to addiction, it applies broadly to people who need to be needed and therefore encourage others to be overly reliant on them. Many children who grow up in households where abuse and addiction are prevalent learn that one way to get positive attention is to be helpful. Caretaking behaviors are rewarded and therefore reinforced. After all, who doesn't like to be on the receiving end of positive affirmation and gratitude? These reinforced behaviors carry over into adulthood where there is a tendency toward helping professions, including ministry. While some helping professions, such as medicine and mental health, have explicit boundaries that limit codependent behavior, the same is not true for clergy, whose contact with parishioners on a personal level is not discouraged but rather expected. This makes it harder to rein in the impulse to become overly involved in the lives of congregants. Clergy who try to be all things to all people are rewarded by being liked and appreciated, but the downside of creating a cycle of dependency is an enormous workload that will ultimately break down under pressure.

Part of the problem is that the Bible often seems to reinforce codependent behavior. Scriptures that emphasize service and personal sacrifice, when misinterpreted, seem to give permission for codependency. However, as is often the case, the Bible can also be confusing. In Galatians, Paul says, "Bear one another's burdens, and in this way you will fulfill the law of Christ."[3] However, just two verses later, he writes, "All must test their own work; then that work, rather than their neighbor's work, will become a cause for pride. For all must carry their own loads."[4] So which is it? Are we to bear the burdens of another or make them carry their own load?

Perhaps the answer lies in the distinction between caretaking versus caring for. When you caretake, you take on the responsibility of meeting the needs of others instead of supporting them as they seek to be responsible for finding ways to meet their own needs. When you care for someone,

3. Gal 6:2.
4. Gal 6:4–5.

you listen, encourage, and support them, offering advice only when it is solicited and letting them take it from there. When you caretake, you are so focused on the needs of others that you fail to meet or even recognize your own needs. When you caretake, you often control and manipulate, expecting others to follow your counsel and becoming offended and even angry if they don't. Caring for means realizing that you can't fix everything. Parker Palmer uses the phrase "functional atheism" to describe people who talk a good game about putting their trust in God while acting as though nothing positive will happen unless they are the ones who make it happen.[5] This way of functioning in the world prevents us from getting out of the way and giving God the space in which to work. Perhaps there are friends or loved ones who would better meet the needs of the person who is hurting. Perhaps this person just needs to be empowered to take the necessary steps toward healing on their own. Following are some guidelines that may be helpful in recovering from the codependency habit.

Know your limits. A clergy friend of mine I'll call Peter had grown up with an emotionally abusive father that he continually tried to please without success. He had been in ministry for several years and acquired a Doctor of Ministry degree along the way, successfully leading two thriving congregations, when he was appointed to a church in an area with a significantly different culture. Peter was stepping into the shoes of a beloved pastor who was leaving to be the district superintendent of the same district in which this church was located. Wanting desperately to fit in, to be accepted, and to gain the approval of his new congregation, he said yes to far more requests for his time and attention than any pastor could possibly accomplish, and in the process, laid himself open to disappointing far more people than he impressed. Ultimately, some of Peter's disgruntled parishioners complained to his supervisor, and he was in danger of losing his appointment. Fortunately, my friend was wise enough to seek help. He found an excellent therapist who helped him recognize that the dynamics of his family of origin were being repeated in his ministry. Through the healing work of therapy, Peter began to be more realistic about what he could and could not accomplish and practiced placing limits on the number of requests to which he committed himself. Through hard work and determination, he was able to turn things around and remained in that church for another three years.

5. Palmer, *Let Your Life Speak,* 64.

Stay in your lane. During a boundaries class I was teaching, a clergy-woman named Claire related a story about a young adult woman who had disclosed an episode of child sexual abuse to her. The woman had been raped by her grandfather at the age of twelve, and she had never told a soul until this moment. As she shared her story, Claire listened with compassion and presence. When the woman stood up to leave, she asked if she could stop by Claire's office from time to time to further process her abuse. Claire assured her that she could, and so began a journey of several years and a total of forty visits in which the rape survivor retold and processed her story. Eventually, she married, had children, and led a happy and fruitful life.

In contrast, I know a pastor, Linda, who discovered that one of her parishioners had suffered profound physical and sexual abuse by several different perpetrators during her childhood. Linda practically adopted this young woman, meeting with her at least twice a week for two hours or more, finding her a therapist, even at times accompanying her to therapy, spending days off with her, going shopping or sharing meals together, and disclosing deeply personal details of her own life. Needless to say, this parishioner became extremely dependent on her pastor and had an extreme reaction when Linda moved to another city.

The difference between these two stories is striking. Claire seemed to know instinctively that her job was to provide pastoral care through compassionate listening and a reliable presence. She never offered more than the woman asked for, which was just an occasional visit to the office to process her abuse with someone she trusted. Linda, on the other hand, took over responsibility for her parishioner's healing and became too involved, even to the point of a personal relationship that was obvious to other members of the congregation. Her codependent engagement with the young woman stepped far beyond the bounds of her role as a provider of pastoral care. This begs the question, who was this really for—the congregant or the pastor? It is so important to have a clear idea of what your role is with the people in your church. What is your job? Whose needs are being met by your over-engagement with someone? Once you've figured that out, be vigilant about staying within the boundaries of what is required of you and what is not.

Let go of expected outcomes. Most of us tend to get attached to desired outcomes and feel disappointed or upset if things don't turn out the way we had hoped. This is especially true for people who are codependent. When they are in rescue or fixing mode, their ego is tied up in planning a course of action, doing everything they can to micro-manage the situation, and achieving the prescribed happy ending. In doing so, they expect to reap the reward of the other person's gratitude and praise for "saving" them. If their advice is not followed, or if a different option is chosen than the one offered, they feel slighted, offended, and taken advantage of. Their thoughts might go something like, "How dare they take up my time with their troubles and then completely ignore my suggestions! If they're not going to follow through on my advice, I am done with them! They can just find someone else to tell their sob story to." This may sound a bit extreme, but it is a common thought pattern for someone who is codependent.

Letting go is hard, especially when codependence is the only reality a person has ever known. It's hard to let go of the ego boost that comes from having people depend on you and tell you how wonderful you are. Letting go of control is a frightening prospect! Admitting that there might be outcomes you can't predict or control is not something codependents easily embrace. Nonetheless, it's important to stop acting as though you are general manager of the universe and let God be God. Following is a list of mantras for those who have difficulty with the idea of letting go of outcomes.

- To let go doesn't mean I don't care; it just means that I can't control another.

- To let go is not to enable, but to allow learning from natural consequences.

- To let go is to admit powerlessness, which means the outcome is not in my hands.

- To let go is not to fix, but to be supportive. It is not to judge, but to allow another to be a human being who makes mistakes.

- To let go is not to be in the middle, arranging all the outcomes, but to allow others to affect their own destinies.

- To let go is not to abandon the other, but to permit them to face reality.

- To let go is to trust God with the outcomes and know that God is present even when things go awry.

Pray first! There was a time a few years ago when I was emerging from a period of extreme over-commitment and exhaustion. It was severe enough that I was determined to prevent that from happening again. I had said "yes" to one too many projects and found myself tied to a one-year contract, doing work that I didn't really enjoy or find life-giving. The "yes" had come about because I didn't engage in a discernment process or listen to my own inner wisdom. I said "yes," because I was needed. Being told that I was the only person that could do this job was just too much of a temptation. Throughout that year, the adage that spoke to me was, "Act in haste, repent at leisure." In the aftermath of that time, I took two days of retreat to ponder how I might do things differently in the future. I spent time in contemplation, seeking God's wisdom for the unfolding of my vocation. As I opened myself up to the Spirit's guidance, the words that came to me were, "Pray first."

What that meant to me was, when I am invited to lead a retreat, give a workshop, serve on a committee, organize a task force, or make any other long-term commitment, I need to pray first before ever accepting the invitation. And I don't mean a quick "Hey God, what do you think?" I'm talking about time spent in listening—to God, to self, to the people who know me best. This includes asking myself why I want to do this, how it will affect my current commitments and my family, and whether this feels like it is congruent with my sense of call. I also try to check in with my body to discern whether there is energy around this invitation or whether I just feel tired when I think about it. If I had done this in the first place, that regretted "Yes" would have been a "No, but thank you for thinking of me."

In terms of requests from your congregation, there are other things you might ask in this time of prayer and discernment. One of the first questions, which I mentioned earlier, might be, "Whose problem is this?" Recalling the "box of self" we looked at, it will become clear to you where the responsibility lies for a specific situation. When you refuse to step into a problem that is not yours, you model healthy boundaries for your congregation. Another important question, related to the first is, "Is this in my job description?" If not, you can be kind but firm in your response, for example, "I'm sorry you're having that problem. That's really not my bailiwick, but here are a couple of resources you could explore." And even if it is in your job description, such as pastoral care, you can clarify your limits and remind yourself of the healthy boundaries that keep you from falling into codependent behavior. And it's always acceptable to delegate!

If, in your discernment process, you find that you really want to accept a request for your time and attention, ask yourself why. Parker Palmer tells about a time when he held a clearness committee to help him discern whether or not he should accept an offer to serve as president of a small educational institution. One of the people in the circle asked him what he would like most about this position. After listing a number of things he *wouldn't* like about the job, Palmer finally said, "I guess what I'd like most is getting my picture in the paper with the word 'president' under it."[6] Needless to say, he did not accept the position! Uncovering your true motives can speak profoundly about what your response to a request should be.

This kind of self-reflection takes times, therefore the corollary to "Pray first" is to never give an immediate response to people who are asking for more from you. Find a way to delay long enough to allow you to undergo this prayerful (and sometimes painful) process of discernment. It can be as simple as, "I need to consult my calendar," or "I need to check with my family." You can tell them you don't have time to talk about it at that moment and commit to getting back to them in a few days, or that you will call them later to get more details—whatever it takes to buy yourself time to reflect.

Codependency is a hard habit to break, but it is possible. It requires being brutally honest with yourself, becoming aware of what it costs you to continue this way of relating to others, and the consistent and careful exercise of learning about and setting healthy boundaries. Boundaries paradoxically create a deeper freedom within the limits of what is appropriate and true to your authentic self.

Reflection Questions

1. What boundary is the most difficult for you to maintain? Reflect on a situation in which boundaries played a key role. How did you handle it? If you had the opportunity for a "do-over," what would you do differently?

2. What new policies would you like to set for yourself?

3. What are the spoken or unspoken expectations in your current church? How might you begin to address some of the unhealthy expectations?

4. Identify a situation in which triangulation was present. How did you handle it? What, if anything, would you have done differently?

5. Do you identify yourself as codependent? What was the source of this behavior? When does your codependency get most triggered? How can you begin to change those behaviors?

6. Palmer, *Let Your Life Speak,* 46.

6

Befriending the Body

For you created my inmost being; you knit me together in my mother's womb. I praise you because I am fearfully and wonderfully made.

—Psalm 139:13–14a (NIV)

The Struggle

Sometimes I think that most of us live from the neck up. We go about our daily lives, frantically trying to accomplish everything on the to-do list, with zero awareness of our bodies. When we are too busy, we ignore hunger and fullness signals, minor aches and pains, tension, and all the other signals our body sends out in an attempt to grab our attention. We fail to actually *inhabit* our bodies! We neglect our physical needs and symptoms and then act surprised when our bodies break down on us, suddenly grabbing our attention with medical conditions that threaten to disrupt the status quo. In her book *Mad Church Disease,* Ann Jackson reports that 69 percent of clergy are overweight, and 83 percent acknowledge unhealthy eating habits.[1] Clergy gulp down fast food on the run, often skip meals entirely, and struggle to find time for fitness activities. Poor dietary habits compromise the immune system and exacerbate stress. It seems like we take better care of our cars than we do our bodies! Everybody knows that when your car starts knocking, you need to get it to the mechanic, but we fail to listen to our body signals enough to recognize when something is wrong. Even worse, we forget that they are sacred vessels.

1. Gauger and Christie, *Clergy Stress,* 28.

Many spiritual writers over the centuries have spoken of the spiritual nature of the human form. Paul reminds us in First Corinthians that our body is a temple of the Holy Spirit,[2] and John O'Donohue similarly suggests that our bodies are "a sacred threshold . . . suffused with wild and vital divinity."[3] Perhaps one of my favorite descriptions of the connection between our bodies and the Holy comes from Julian of Norwich, "For as the body is clad in the cloth, and the flesh in the skin, and the bones in the flesh, and the heart in the trunk, so are we, soul and body, clad and enclosed in the goodness of God."[4]

Of course, part of the difficulty with perceiving our body as sacred is the multitude of messages with which we are bombarded on a daily basis, messages that revere only slender and fit bodies. Societal norms dictate that ideal female bodies must be slim, but with curves in the right places, and ideal male bodies are muscular and flat-bellied. If we're being honest, very few of us fit into those categories. On rare occasions, we hear messages that encourage us to accept whatever shape our body is in, acknowledging that people come in all shapes and sizes. If we can manage it, this feels great for a while, right up until the time the doctor looks up from our medical chart and says gravely, "It's time for you to lose some weight."

In addition to the mixed messages we hear from our culture, some of us also received mixed messages about body image and food in our families of origin. How many of us were encouraged to clean our plates when we were young? Or to eat whatever was put in front of us whether we liked it or not? This was certainly the case in my own family as a child. At the same time as this was happening, I was keenly aware of how negatively my father viewed people who were overweight. Whenever he saw someone who was on the heavy side, he would make derogatory comments about their size and/or eating habits. Of course, my father had the metabolism of a horse and could eat whatever he wanted without gaining an ounce. When I asked him many years later about his prejudice against people who were overweight, he said he thought they had no self-control. I pointed out that not everyone has his metabolism, but I wish I had asked how children are supposed to develop self-control when the quantity of food they eat is dictated by their parents. It's tough to pay attention to your body signals around hunger and fullness when that's how you grew

2. 1 Cor 6:19.

3. O'Donohue, *Anam Cara*, 47–48.

4. See Wiseman, "Body in Spiritual Practice," 9.

up. As an adult, how do you resolve the conflict between eating everything on your plate as you were taught while trying desperately to avoid putting on those dreaded extra pounds?

Another equally troublesome rule or message is the admonition to "Be polite" when dining in other people's homes. Some cooks love to create huge meals and encourage their guests to take second and even third helpings in order to reassure themselves that their efforts were appreciated. This is yet another situation in which we learn to ignore our body's own signals about food intake. It is particularly difficult for clergy, who are often in situations where food has been cooked or provided by others—the multitude of potlucks, the donuts at morning meetings, the cookies at evening meetings, or the invitations to dine with parishioners. When you haven't had a chance to eat all day, and the food is there in front of you, with the "Be polite" rule echoing in your head, how are you to resist?

I think the best place to start is with this idea of befriending one's body. In his seminal book *The Road Less Traveled*, Scott Peck introduced a definition of love that I found intriguing. He suggested that genuine love is the "will to extend one's self for the purpose of nurturing one's own or another's (growth and well-being)."[5] Couldn't this apply to loving our own bodies as well? If we truly love our bodies, we accept whatever shape they are in, the particular physical traits that we inherited from our mothers, fathers, grandparents, or our Uncle Harold, because those are things we can't change. And then we look at the health of our body, things like weight, cholesterol levels, blood pressure, body mass index, et cetera, and we ask ourselves, "What would be the best thing for my body's well-being?" Perhaps this is what Barbara Brown Taylor meant when she wrote, "It is time to do a better job of wearing my skin with gratitude instead of loathing."[6] Can we be grateful for the things our body does for us and decide to treat it better instead of ignoring it completely, except for when we get on the scale and curse at the number we see? What would that look like?

The first thing we can do is stop calling our body names like the school bully in fifth grade. The terms we use to describe our bodies are often quite pejorative. Over my many years of working with therapy clients, I've heard people say things like, "I'm such a cow," "I've gotta get rid of this spare tire around my waist," and "Ugh, look at this muffin top." The language we use in reference to our bodies invariably infects the way we feel about ourselves.

5. Peck, *Road Less Traveled*, 81.
6. Taylor, *Altar in the World*, 38.

And if the only voice we allow ourselves to hear is the inner critic, we are sunk before we even start on the path toward a healthier body. Self-criticism leads to discouragement leads to frustration leads to emotional eating. Back to square one. If we must talk about the current state of our bodies, perhaps we could use more accurate and non-critical language, like "I weigh a few pounds more than I'd like to right now," or a forward-looking statement such as, "I'm in the process of creating a healthier body."

Food

When beginning any kind of health plan (after first consulting with your doctor), it is helpful to be your own cheerleader by choosing an affirmation to repeat to yourself regularly. Good affirmations avoid any negative statements about your body and are focused on the process of becoming, rather than your current condition or a specific end goal. You want a statement that reminds you of the process so you can continue to live into that process daily and give yourself encouragement, even on the hard days. Ideally, a health plan doesn't stop when you achieve your goal weight or ideal blood pressure or cholesterol numbers. Good affirmations help to emphasize this. Below are some suggested affirmations, but the best ones are those you create yourself.

- "I am treating my body with love and respect."
- "Every day I am creating a healthier and more radiant body."
- "I am working daily to make the temple of my body healthier and stronger."
- "I bless my body with healthy food, exercise, and rest."
- "I love myself, body and soul, and offer all that I am to God."
- "I am grateful for my body and devote myself to its renewal and health."

The prophet Isaiah writes, "Why do you spend your money for that which is not bread, and your labor for that which does not satisfy? Listen carefully to me, and eat what is good."[7] While this is often interpreted in a more metaphorical way, it doesn't have to be. Wouldn't it be great to consider the kinds of foods that are good for your body and that also satisfy your

7. Isa 55:2.

palate? When I read this passage, I think about the natural foods with which God has blessed us. An abundance of fruit and vegetables and whole grains are often far preferable to the processed foods that contain preservatives and added ingredients. There are so many options available now that are both healthy and tasty. Feeding your body these things is one step in the goal of recognizing and treating your body as a sacred trust.

In the book *Intuitive Eating*, authors Tribole and Resch, one a registered dietitian and the other a nutritional therapist, write about the downside of dieting. They believe that diets ultimately fail, citing both the physiological and psychological effects of food restriction. Instead, they recommend that no foods be labeled as bad or off limits. This just sets up an automatic desire for the food in question. After all, God told Adam and Eve not to eat the fruit, and look what happened! Instead, they recommend that you learn to pay closer attention to your body's signals of hunger and fullness. In other words, eat when you are hungry; don't wolf your food down, but eat with intention, noticing when you are satisfied. Then stop. It's easier to do this when you aren't watching television, conducting a meeting, or playing games on your mobile device at the same time.

It's also important to notice when you are feeding your emotions rather than your body. Many of us engage in emotional eating on a regular basis. Twelve-step programs have an acronym for the times when we are likely to relapse from any kind of addiction—HALT—which stands for hungry, angry, lonely, or tired. There are many more emotions that can lead us to ingest food when our body doesn't really need it, such as boredom or stress, but this handy reminder can be helpful. It reminds us not to allow ourselves to get too hungry before eating. If we go past hungry to ravenous, we are not going to be judicious about what we put in our mouths. We are going to eat more rapidly and miss the cues that might tell us when we're satisfied. The easily remembered acronym can also remind us that emotional eating isn't healthy eating. When I'm heading to the refrigerator or cupboard because I am upset, it's not celery that I'm after. It's cake or ice cream or potato chips or anything calorie-laden.

So when we are in need of comfort food, what do we do that doesn't either completely deny ourselves or make us feel guilty in the aftermath of a binge? I think it's about paying attention, recognizing that you are not physiologically hungry and asking yourself what that's about. Why are you wanting food at this moment? What is the emotion that is driving you into the kitchen? Once you have identified the emotion, ask yourself if the food is really going to help. The reality is, probably not. Okay, sure, it will spur a little rush of dopamine that will temporarily make you feel better, but the guilt will erase that benefit in short order. And in the meantime, nothing has changed about the feelings that you are hoping to cover up with food. Instead of eating, maybe you can process those emotions via journaling, talking to a good friend, going for a walk, or taking a relaxing bath. Find other things that give you comfort. Prayer and contemplation can shift your perspective and help you let go of what's troubling you.

Now, let's look at the life of clergy and the special problems that make loving your body so much more difficult. One former pastor of mine would often go all day without eating or drinking because she was so busy. The unfortunate side effect of that was that she would occasionally get light-headed and dizzy, even passing out at the most inopportune moments. The schedule of a pastor is not remotely nine to five. It is unpredictable and hectic and no respecter of traditional meal times. The key to resolving this dilemma is planning. Always carry healthy snacks in your car—fruit, nuts, protein bars, etc. Hydrate as much as possible. Identify the fast food places that offer low-fat, low-calorie options that are located along your frequent routes to and from the hospital, church, parsonage, et cetera. If there are people in the congregation who invariably bring sweet treats to meetings, ask them to include some healthier options. Conduct a health campaign in the church, and suggest that potlucks include some dishes that are low-calorie and low-fat. This will also be helpful to parishioners who have health issues such as diabetes, high blood pressure, high cholesterol, or other chronic medical conditions.

Fitness

Of course, any health plan includes more than just healthy eating. Your body needs movement and exercise. Unfortunately, we get hung up on the idea that we must set aside thirty minutes or an hour of continuous exercise daily in order to be fit. We conjure up images of sweating it out at the gym, power walking five miles, or swimming laps at the local pool. While any of these activities would be good for you, they aren't always realistic for clergy whose schedules are less regular and predictable than most. It may be necessary for you to get creative and let go of pre-conceived notions that exercise should happen at specific places and times.

One pastor that I was working with in therapy was bemoaning how hard it was to fit exercise into his day. His mornings were always a mad dash to help his wife fix breakfast and get the kids off to school. Then it was usually out the door for a meeting or a hospital visitation before his office hours began. As he talked, it became clear that he was operating under the belief that exercise was something one could only do first thing in the morning. When I challenged him on this, his eyes got wide. "I could keep my bicycle at the church and go cycling at lunch!" It was such a simple thing, but it made a huge difference.

Some pastors ride their bikes or walk to work as often as possible. Some purposefully block out times for exercise on their calendar and place strict boundaries on that time. Others sneak in fifteen minutes of yoga or tai-chi whenever they can, finding that it's easier to take advantage of those occasional fifteen-minute gaps in the schedule than larger blocks of time. Then they schedule longer sessions of physical activity on their Sabbath. One clergy spouse recommends walking around the sanctuary for fifteen minutes a couple of times a day or, even more drastic, vacuuming the church! Sometimes cleaning is a nice change from the mental and spiritual responsibilities of the clergy life, and it's good exercise too. A friend of mine suggested that clergy could institute "Walk and Talk," a time when parishioners can visit with their pastor while walking together when weather permits. Not only does that give both clergy and lay people an opportunity for healthy activity, it creates a more informal atmosphere for sharing dreams and concerns for the church.

Whatever you choose to do, it's always better to find activities that you enjoy so that you will actually *want* to do them rather than forcing yourself to do something that you hate. The important thing is to move. Exercise is an essential piece of loving and caring for your body. It's also important not to get discouraged when you experience days or even longer periods of time where fitting in exercise just seems impossible. We all have those times when things happen that are out of our control, and our best-laid plans fall by the wayside. When this happens, it's important to give yourself grace and then begin again. We are an Easter people after all, and every day is a new beginning.

Sleep

Another key piece of the puzzle is giving your body the rest it needs. Many clergy are chronically sleep deprived. Not only is this counter-productive to health, but it's also dangerous. Experts say there is no difference between driving while sleep deprived and driving under the influence. My sister is a retired clergywoman who for years was buckling under a huge load of sleep debt. She could fall asleep anywhere, anytime. There are hundreds of movies that she only saw the beginnings of. She could fall asleep during a hockey game or sitting bolt upright while studying Greek flashcards in the car (thankfully her husband was driving). There was always more to do, and rather than prioritizing and letting go of the less important tasks, she tried to do it all, regardless of what time it was. Nights with only five hours of sleep were commonplace. Then something shifted, and she realized that she couldn't continue to do this to herself. Maybe she realized that the quality of the work she did while sleep-deprived was considerably less than what she was able to accomplish when well-rested. Or perhaps she figured out that it's really hard to be fully present to the people of your congregation when all you want to do is put your head on your desk and close your eyes. Whatever it was, she finally made a commitment to get to bed by ten or eleven every night, and the difference was remarkable.

Sleep hygiene is extremely important. It involves trying to go to bed and get up at the same time every day, sleeping in a dark and cool room, and gradually dimming the lights in your home starting about an hour before you go to bed. Limiting caffeine intake after mid-day is also essential. Caffeine has a half-life of seven hours. This means that seven hours after caffeine is consumed, half of it is still in your body. And seven hours after *that*, half of the half is still present. So if you drink your coffee at eight o'clock in the morning, a quarter of the caffeine is still in your body at ten o'clock that night. While you may think that caffeine doesn't affect you, it does. You may fall asleep out of sheer fatigue, but the quality of your sleep will be reduced due to the caffeine remaining in your system.

Touch

One final word about balanced care of the body—we all need to experience the healing power of touch. Not only is touch pleasurable to the body and an important part of many relationships, touch strengthens the immune system. It's so easy to rush through our busy days without the benefit of human touch. Hugs with parishioners are a complicated subject in today's increased awareness of the need to respect boundaries, so some clergy make it a rule not to hug at all. And even clergy who are married or partnered can go days without physical contact with their loved ones solely due to conflicting schedules and lack of time. In the Hebrew tradition, one of the acceptable and even recommended activities on the Sabbath is lovemaking. Some might even consider it spiritual practice. Sexual contact is one of our most basic human needs, and clergy are not exempt from this reality. For single clergy, other sources of touch become even more essential. Therapeutic massage is an excellent source of touch and a good way to invest in self-care. Playing with or cuddling your pet can also be a means of satisfying the need for touch. Good friends and colleagues can be relied upon for a comforting hug when needed, and even a good bubble bath or soak in the hot tub will fill the bill.

Spiritual Practice

Barbara Brown Taylor posits that "every spiritual practice begins with the body."[8] If this is so, then our body is an essential means of grace for connecting with the Divine in all of life. And when we involve our body in spiritual practice, we are also blessing and being blessed by this human vessel we walk the earth in. There are myriad different body prayers to be derived from different faith traditions. From Catholicism, we can use genuflection and the sign of the cross as body prayers. From the Orthodox tradition, we glean special prayer postures, such as seated with head and shoulders bowed. This is an ideal position for the reciting of the Jesus Prayer, "Lord Jesus Christ, have mercy on me, a sinner." This prayer is prayed in rhythm with the breath—yet another way we pray with our bodies. There are also specific prayers that are recited and accompanied by meaningful body gestures, such as "Six Gestures for the Morning Praise" from Joyce Rupp's book, *Out of the Ordinary.*[9] Some people pray in the prone position, either face down in penitence and humility or face up with arms spread wide, opening the soul to God. Native Americans also pray face down on the earth, celebrating creation and the expansive God who called the world into being.

8. Taylor, *Altars in the World*, 40.
9. Rupp, *Out of the Ordinary*, 171.

I love the Old Testament story of David bringing the Ark of the Covenant up to Jerusalem. "David danced before the LORD with all his might . . . and all the house of Israel brought up the ark of the LORD with shouting, and with the sound of the trumpet."[10] Now that is about as embodied as prayer can get! Sometimes I think our bodies more eloquently express our deepest feelings, whether joy or sorrow, far better than our words ever could. During a spiritual-formation event I attended several years ago, a woman was brought in to teach us sacred circle dancing. We had a delightful time, laughing at our initial clumsiness, reveling in the movement of our bodies, and finally awakening to the sacredness of the music and the dance. So whether you dance in the privacy of your own home or at a communal event, be aware of the spiritual nature of dancing to the rhythms of the soul.

One last example of body prayer is walking the labyrinth. Originally designed in the Middle Ages for Christians who were unable to make a pilgrimage to the Holy Land, it is a walking meditation for those on a spiritual quest. While there are many different configurations for a labyrinth, the most widely known is the labyrinth that was built into the stone floor of the Chartres Cathedral in France. It bears some resemblance to a maze but has no dead ends. The path always leads to the center, which is understood to be the heart of God. As one walks the labyrinth, the mind is quieted and the soul opened to hear the inner promptings of the Spirit. The inner journey is one of receptivity, while the outward journey is the gathering of strength and energy to go out into the world having been given wisdom and insight through the presence of God. If you are not aware of any labyrinths near you, you can do a search on labyrinthlocator.com.

I often think of creation as God's playground. The more we can connect with the natural world around us, the more closely we feel connected to God. Thus, walking or hiking in nature becomes embodied spiritual practice. This also pertains to activities such as kayaking, swimming, beachcombing, cross-country skiing—any physical activity that brings us into intimate contact with the earth and sky. Sometimes, even taking our shoes off and walking barefoot on the earth is enough to connect us with the spiritual realm as well as the dirt or grass beneath our feet. These are also ways in which we treat our bodies with love and care. We might suffer aches and pains the next day, but they are good aches and pains, indicative of our bodies need to move and honor God at the same time.

10. 2 Sam 6:14–15.

Another good reason for taking care of our bodies is that, as clergy, you are the hands and feet of God in the world. Karl Barth says, "To fold the hands in prayer is the beginning of an uprising against the disorder of the world."[11] If we want to be a part of that uprising, we need healthy bodies to visit the sick, feed the poor, and advocate for justice for the disadvantaged and the disenfranchised. Of his experience of marching for civil rights in Alabama with Martin Luther King, Jr., Rabbi Abraham Heschel said, "My feet were praying."[12] With the renewed vigor of a healthy body, one that we have befriended and treated with love, we are called to pray with our hands and feet in this hurting and troubled world.

Reflection Questions

1. What were the explicit or implicit messages about body weight in your family of origin?

2. What is your biggest psychological barrier to becoming more healthy?

3. What are your triggers for emotional eating, and how might you interrupt the cycle?

4. What are you already doing to improve your fitness level? Name one activity you think you could add without a major revision of your schedule.

5. What is the current quantity and quality of sleep you are getting? How does lack of sleep impact your ability to function?

6. How might embodied spiritual practice change your attitude toward your body?

11. Kark Barth, as quoted in Kenneth Leech, *True Prayer* (San Francisco: Harper and Row, 1968).

12. See Ryan, "Positive Spirituality of Body," 41.

7

Water from the Rock

Spiritual Practice for the Twenty-First Century

Then when you call upon me and come and pray to me, I will hear you. When you search for me, you will find me; if you seek me with all your heart, I will let you find me, says the LORD.

—JEREMIAH 29:12–14A

Among the myriad duties and demands of ministry, one of the easiest things to set aside or put off is one's spiritual life. There's just no time. Spiritual reading is limited to Scripture and other resources in preparation for Sunday's sermon. Prayer is often focused on intercessory prayer for congregants and others or writing the pastoral prayer for Sunday worship. A day of true Sabbath might occur once a month or even less. The result is that many of the clergy members I work with experience spiritual dryness. Over time this can lead to a sense of guilt and anxiety over what might be perceived as a lack of authenticity. Church members look to their pastors as an example of living the spiritual life, and yet the sad truth might be that the laity are engaging in spiritual practice more often than their pastor.

The number-one problem is time. Our clergy are too busy. This is compounded by the fact that we live in a culture that has an addiction to urgency, so much so that most of us spend our days in a mad dash for the finish line, and then we wonder what we actually accomplished. And yet there is a longing to close the divide between the mundane and the holy. We want, as John Wesley did, to have not just a devotional *time* but a devotional *life!* The question is, how does one listen for the "still, small voice" of God in the midst of all the clamoring voices that compete for your time? At times it must feel as though you are trying to get water from the rock without the aid of Moses' staff!

However, it would be a mistake to believe that the only thing standing between you and a satisfying spiritual life is time. Another barrier can be the mistaken belief that the spiritual realm is difficult to access and that we need to go to a beautiful sanctuary or retreat center or other special place in order to experience union with God. After living in the desert for twenty-two years, barren places are normally not the kind of scenery that draws me into spiritual space. Now that I live in Washington, I have lots of opportunity to commune with nature in the forests, mountains, lakes, and ocean beaches that are plentiful in this beautiful state. But the center of the state is decidedly desert-like. Other than in spring, its plains and hills are brown and sere, in other words, not remotely conducive to a spiritual moment in my opinion. But one day I was driving through such an area of stark landscapes to visit my aging father, and I took a route that wound through the deep coulees that had been gouged out by the Ice Age flood of Lake Missoula. As I drove through these chasms, I was suddenly aware of the power of our Creator. It was almost as if I could hear God's voice rolling like thunder through the canyons and dry river beds. I was transported in that moment to a sublime sense of union with the Divine. It was as though God was in the car with me, and we shared in the wonder of it all.

The coulees on Highway 2 became a doorway to the kingdom of God for me that day. Jesus tells us that the kingdom of heaven is near. I think he was not just talking about time, but about space. The portal to the kingdom is within our reach, *right here, all around us.* Any place can be a thin space, a threshold between the daily and the holy, a place where they come together. I believe that heaven is merely another dimension that intersects with our world by means of a threshold that is always present and that we may cross whenever we fix our minds upon God. Rabbi Mendel of Kotzk once said, "God is only where you let Him in."[1]

Donald Shockley is one of many writers that speak of this practice of seeing God in the daily places and events of our lives. Over time, Shockley cultivated the spiritual practice of watching while waiting. Waiting in restaurants, doctor's offices, airports, parks, and more were opportunities to see God in the people and incidents that unfolded around him. He learned to take in his surroundings with new eyes, and wrote down his spiritual

1 Wikiquote (website), "Menachem Mendel."

insights on receipts, napkins, envelopes or anything he could get his hands on. Ultimately, friends and members of his congregations urged him to put these meditations into a book, which became *Private Prayers in Public Places*. For clergy who often have to "hurry up and wait" in hospitals, coffee shops, and traffic, perhaps this spiritual practice of watching while waiting could become a source of insight and renewal for you.

Another obstacle to the spiritual life is our rigid separation between what is sacred and what is secular. This unnecessarily shortens the list of spiritual practices. For a long time after I had read Marjorie Thompson's wonderful book *Soul Feast*, I mistakenly believed that the eight spiritual practices she described there were a finite list. But that book was a starting place for me that ultimately took me to the two-year Academy for Spiritual Formation, which opened my eyes to a broad array of spiritual disciplines. Over time, I have come to believe that the only difference between the sacred and secular is one of intention. When the intention of turning our hearts and minds toward God is present, even a game of golf can be sacred!

A few years ago, friends of ours came to visit and had found out about a bluegrass concert that was taking place in a community near us. They wanted to go, and we agreed to go with them even though we weren't big bluegrass fans. However, as I sat in the small auditorium, listening to the band's joyful music flowing over me, it occurred to me that this might be the sound of God laughing. Suddenly, the concert was transformed from a hospitable obligation into spiritual practice.

Kathleen Norris, in her book *The Quotidian Mysteries*, describes a Catholic wedding she attended once. It was a full Mass, and afterwards she noticed that part of the ritual was the cleaning of the chalice and paten. The presiding priest was literally doing the dishes! This idea of an everyday household chore being liturgy intrigued her. "Homage was being paid to the lowly truth that we human beings must wash the dishes after we eat and drink. . . . And I found it enormously comforting to see the priest as a kind of daft housewife, overdressed for the kitchen, in bulky robes, puttering about the altar, washing up after having served so great a meal to so many people."[2] She began to explore the idea that our daily chores, the mundane and menial tasks of life, could be turned into liturgy. Just like Brother Lawrence centuries before her, she discovered that laundry, peeling potatoes, dusting, and all those other tedious tasks that contribute to the shared life of our families and communities could be transformed into a gift and a way

2. Norris, *Quotidian Mysteries*, 3.

of offering ourselves to God and others. The difference between tedium and spiritual practice is intention!

What this stirs in me is the idea that spiritual practice doesn't have to always be time set apart. It can be added to what we're already doing, like an overlay on top of other daily tasks that don't necessarily require our full attention. All we need to do is start thinking outside the proverbial box! While the maxim is trite and overused, it does speak to a deeper truth. We often get stuck in a box of our own making, especially with our fixed ideas about what we *should* be doing and how we're supposed to do it.

Many of my spiritual-direction clients share the belief that spiritual practice is something to be done first thing in the morning for a full hour and involves the study of Scripture followed by a time of prayer for all the people on their "prayer list." When I introduce the radical idea that prayer can happen anywhere at any time, they are astonished, then intrigued, then excited. When the old "shoulds" fall away, space is opened up for new possibilities for connecting with the Holy. Begin exploring some of your own basic assumptions about not only the nature of spiritual practice but your beliefs about when, where, and how that should happen.

Let's take a look at some of the typical activities that occupy your days, especially the ones that don't require concentrated thought. The idea is to view those activities as opportunities for prayer, liturgy, or contemplation. For example, most of the pastors I know spend a *lot* of time in their cars. My earlier story of driving through the coulees in central Washington is just one example of how driving can become spiritual practice. Mindfulness while driving can help you notice not only the traffic and traffic signs you need to pay attention to but also the things that are often invisible when your mind is preoccupied with worries and to-do lists. You might notice an act of kindness by someone on the sidewalk, a homeless person in need of prayer, or a tree growing out of a crack in the sidewalk, speaking of resiliency and hope. City traffic also provides many opportunities for prayer at stoplights and in traffic jams. You might pray for members of your congregation or fellow travelers on the road, or try a breath prayer that connects you to the rhythm of your breath and the breath of God.[3]

Breath prayer consists of a short phrase that names the God to which you pray, such as "loving God," "gentle Spirit," or "divine Healer," and a short petition that states what you are most in need of at that moment. The first

3. You will find some sample prayers, litanies, and other spiritual helps in Appendices B and C.

phrase is spoken aloud or silently on the inhale, and the petition is repeated on the exhale. For example, an abbreviated version of the Jesus Prayer can be a breath prayer—"Lord Jesus Christ, have mercy on me." Other possibilities might be "Holy Wisdom, guide my path," "Creative God, inspire me," or "Compassionate One, give me peace." The variations are endless. Some people choose one breath prayer that they use as a permanent mantra; others change their breath prayer to meet whatever need is uppermost in their lives at any given time. Personalize your prayer to your own particular needs and your own way of addressing the Divine.

Another way of using your car as a rolling monastery is to listen to contemplative music instead of the news as you drive, whether this be Taize songs, Gregorian chants, or just mellow instrumentals. My favorites are CDs with a combination of music and nature sounds. This puts me in touch with the God of creation and helps me feel the Divine presence that grounds me and gives me peace.

Combining spiritual practice and exercise is another area where you can wrap prayer into something you are hopefully already doing. Most exercise is very rhythmic in nature, so any kind of rhythmic prayer or litany would work well. This would include breath prayer, lines of Scripture, especially psalms, a favorite poem, hymns, et cetera. One of my favorite recitations during times of anxiety or distress is the writing of Julian of Norwich, "All shall be well, and all shall be well. All manner of things shall be well."

These rhythmic practices also work well with activities like household chores, gardening, knitting, and other crafts and hobbies. In a way, adding prayer to these repetitive activities is a little like praying the rosary. When your hands are occupied with an activity that takes little focused attention, it frees the soul to connect with God. Your analytic left brain is busy counting stitches, digging holes, or chopping vegetables, which distracts it from anxious thoughts and "mental popcorn" (those unwelcome thoughts that pop into your head of their own volition). This allows your right brain to expand into the spiritual realm and fly free.

We live in a culture that values critical thinking, analysis, and problem-solving. In this rapidly changing world that relies on communication, we are subject to information overload via the internet, television, cell phones, devices, and long, drawn-out meetings. I once read that we are bombarded with something like 10,000 words a day! While most of this deluge is necessary, it does create an imbalance within us. We spend so much time functioning out of our left brain that we can ultimately find ourselves unable to turn off the obsessive and intrusive thoughts. Without a doubt, the clergy life requires a steady diet of words—words for the church newsletter, words for the sermon, words to prepare for Bible studies and other classes, words to share with those in need of pastoral care. But when we fail to escape the confines of a word-driven society on occasion, we forget that God's primary language is silence. We can only truly hear the Divine when we allow all the words to fall away. The barrier is that clergy are usually highly articulate. They're very comfortable and accomplished with words. It's natural for the ego to hold onto what it's good at, but there are times when we must let go of our reliance on words and listen to the silence in which God speaks.

Sometimes the mode of being we use *least* is the best pathway to God. This is why it's so important to use all of our senses on the spiritual journey, not just our heads. Sensory cues for the holy can be invitations to awareness of God's presence that draw you into a moment of connection with the Divine. This might be prayer beads or a cross hanging from your rearview mirror in the car, an icon or favorite religious painting on your office wall, or a special rock, shell, or leaf in your own sacred space. If you place these items in areas where you will see them often, they can serve as reminders of that spiritual realm that is available whenever you turn your mind toward God. Just a word of caution—you might need to move them occasionally so they don't just blend into the background and become something you don't notice anymore.

Another visual practice you might consider is subscribing to the Upper Room's Sight Psalms, a daily e-mail of beautiful photography paired with a Scripture verse or other spiritual quote. You can do the same on your own with a book of photography or art that you use in the same manner as *Lectio Divina*, pondering how God is speaking to you through the image.[4] If you do find yourself transported into God's presence by words, write favorite Bible verses on index cards or sticky notes and put them on your desk, your mirror, your refrigerator, anywhere they will catch your eye and serve as a portal to the holy.

If you are more auditory than visual, try audio cues such as the chants or music mentioned above. I find that ringing a small chime can help me tune into my spiritual self more readily, enabling me to clear out the thoughts that get in the way of connecting with God. Olfactory cues can also be

---

4. For more information on *Lectio Divina*, check out Appendix B at the back of this book.

helpful—scented candles or incense, a walk through the woods enjoying the scent of the pines, or the smell of cut grass or damp earth after the rain.

Earlier in this chapter I mentioned the practice of mindfulness while driving, but mindfulness is a wonderful practice no matter where you are or what you are doing. It is simply the practice of noticing non-judgmentally. Brother David Steindl-Rast refers to mindfulness as waking up to surprise.[5] He believes that when we open our eyes to the wonders of the world around us, we become more aware of God's superfluous grace. We live in a world of abundance, and yet we hardly ever notice it. Mindfulness leads directly to an overwhelming gratitude for that abundance. It draws us fully into the present moment. Take a few moments right now to stop reading and look mindfully at your surroundings. Don't let anything fade into the woodwork. Even if it's something you look at all the time, try to see it with new eyes. Then notice the gratitude that comes with your awareness of being blessed. This is a spiritual practice that you can do anytime, anywhere, for only a few minutes, but it will make a significant difference in your day.

One of the common difficulties in establishing regular spiritual practice is that we attempt to make it so regimented that we become frustrated with ourselves when we fail to live up to our intentions. Then our spiritual life becomes a list of things we *should* do instead of things we *want* to do, and we end up quitting altogether. The point of spiritual discipline is not to suffocate the soul with rigidity and rules but to give it space in which to bloom and grow. So as you begin to introduce some of the suggestions in this chapter, be gentle with yourself, and don't try to do every one of them all at once. Use variety to keep your spiritual life from getting stale. Know that your spiritual needs will change according to circumstances, mood, and season. Mix up your spiritual reading as well. Instead of a heavy theological treatise, try reading a book of poetry by Mary Oliver, Hafiz, Rumi, Wendell Berry, or one of your own favorites. Sample the writings of Richard Rohr, Terry Hershey, Henry Nouwen, Anne Lamott, Rachel Naomi Remen, or Margaret Silf, among many other great spiritual writers.

As you incorporate these practices into the routine of your days, my hope is that you discover a continual daily awareness of God, a sense of being accompanied by "God with us" at all times and in all places.

5. Steindl-Rast, *Gratefulness*, 9.

Reflection Questions

1. What is the current state of your spiritual life? How often do you engage in spiritual practice? What are your means of grace?

2. What are your internal barriers to spiritual practice?

3. What are the activities, places, and/or times that you have become aware of as opportunities for spiritual practice?

4. Recall a time when God caught you by surprise with a sense of God's presence.

5. How much are you dependent on words in your relationship with God? What is your relationship with silence?

6. Which of your senses most deeply connects you with the Divine?

8

Nurturing Relationships

Companions on the Journey

How very good and pleasant it is when kindred live together in unity! . . . It is like the dew of Hermon, which falls on the mountains of Zion. For there the LORD ordained his blessing, life forevermore.

—PSALM 133:1,3

A few years ago, I was asked to give a plenary address to a gathering of clergy on the topic of wellness. I had often used Jesus' answer to the teacher of the law about which is the greatest commandment—"You shall love the Lord your God with all your heart, and with all your soul, and with all your mind, and with all your strength"[1]—to emphasize the importance of balancing emotional, spiritual, mental, and physical health in a holistic paradigm of wellness. As I pondered what I wanted to say to these clergy men and women, I felt like I needed a good metaphor as a framework for holding it all together. What, I wondered, would be a useful metaphor that all clergy could relate to? It occurred to me that pastors spend more time in their cars than most. The four aspects of self that Jesus referred to in the Great Commandment (mind, strength, heart, spirit) could be the four tires of the car, but still, something was missing. In my mind, the other piece of

1. Mark 12:30.

wellness for clergy is relational, but where does that fit in this metaphor? And then I realized that your relationships are the people in the car with you who can help diagnose a "mechanical" problem or help you change a tire when it goes flat. They can tell when you are too tired or too stressed to drive, and they can hear the sound of your engine when it's not running smoothly and urge you to go get a tune-up.

This felt like a key factor in helping clergy stay healthy throughout their careers in ministry. The ministry is often a lonely job. Surrounded by people, they are nonetheless set apart as the spiritual leader who is there to tend to the needs of others rather than getting their needs met by others. Appropriate boundaries preclude the pastor from forging deep personal relationships with the people of their congregations. Also, some denominations expect their pastors to itinerate, with an average frequency for reappointment of between five to seven years. This regular upheaval disrupts whatever relationships may have been developed within the broader communities they serve. Yet clergy need people in their lives with whom they can experience reciprocity of relationship. Thus, it is essential to cultivate these kinds of relationships—the family, friends, and colleagues who will ride in your car with you through the journey of ministry and help you stay healthy and whole along the way. In this chapter, we will discuss these three groups of life companions, their importance, and how to maintain them.

Friends

Humans are biologically wired to be social beings. From our earliest beginnings, we learned that banding together helped us survive—from prehistoric humans gathered around a fire for warmth and protection, to "circling the wagons," to barn-raisings, we have known that life together is better than life apart. We all need friends on the winding and sometimes perilous path of life. Even introverts need friends. Unfortunately, the life of clergy complicates things. When you live in small communities where everyone knows who you are, it's hard to let down your guard when you know that people are looking to you as a role model for the church. And when you move frequently, it's hard to maintain the friends you've made when distance separates you. In one survey, 57 percent of clergy reported that they did not have any close friends in their community.[2]

2. Gauger and Christie, *Clergy Stress,* 15.

Yet it is particularly helpful for clergy to have friends from outside the church. This is especially important for single or divorced clergy. Friends are the people who can offer a different perspective and can accept you for who you are without filtering their opinion through the expectations of the church. They can see things differently, tell you when a situation is unhealthy, or when you are going off the rails. They might be the first to notice that you are more stressed than usual or slipping into a depression or in deep need of self-care. These kinds of friends provide balance when ministry is sucking the life out of you.

For example, one pastor I know has a group of friends that he bicycles with once a week. While engaged in that shared activity, the subject of church doesn't come up at all. Another female pastor had a long career in the corporate world before she entered into ministry. She still maintains the friendships she gained during that time, because they offer the balance of an outside perspective and allow her to be herself. She doesn't have to censor herself when she is with them. When I was part of a two-year spiritual-formation program several years ago, I had a conversation about dreams with a clergy friend of mine. He reported that a few days before we gathered for our quarterly retreat, he had a dream in which he was in a bar, laughing and having a great time when several members of his congregation walked in. He asked me what I thought that meant. I told him that I imagined it was about the difficulty of "letting one's hair down" as a pastor in his community and that he was looking forward to this time away where he could be himself. Our cohort was a safe place where he was known and accepted. And they were people after his own heart, who were passionate about a deeper walk with God, but could also enjoy his joie de vivre and offbeat sense of humor.

Everyone needs places and people with whom they can "blow off steam." We need people with whom we don't have to choose our words quite so carefully or wonder what kind of impression we're making. This is why friends are so important. The question becomes, how can one overcome some of the obstacles to making friends in a new place or the obstacle of distance when long-time friends are far away? When you are in a new community, you can meet people outside the church by taking a class at the local community college or other organization. Something as simple as walking your dog around the neighborhood is another good way to make the acquaintance of your neighbors. You can strike up a conversation at the local coffee shop, seek out groups that share a common hobby or activity, or volunteer at the local animal shelter or food bank. You can also stay connected with old friends through video chat platforms such as Skype or Facetime, text periodically to say hello, or plan get-togethers every few months or annually, depending on how far apart you live. On the days when you are tired and stressed and don't want to talk to anybody at all, that is probably when you need friends the most. These are some of those folks who are riding in the car of your vocation with you for the long haul. Don't hesitate to reach out and ask for help from people who care about you.

Colleagues

When I first began conducting wellness workshops for clergy several years ago, I was told not to expect a large turnout. When I asked why, the response was, "Because clergy don't want anyone else to know they need help." I was a bit stunned by this statement. It had never occurred to me that there would be so much distrust among colleagues that one couldn't be vulnerable about one's struggles. I have since discovered that this is indeed the reality for many pastors. In fact, lack of collegiality is much more complex than I first understood it to be. Ronald Hagerman describes this complexity well:

> Many clergy are uncomfortable about seeking advice from colleagues, for they find them preoccupied with their own church business, their status, or the ever-present numbers game. Others indicate that they do not find their professional peers to be good listeners. Still others confess that they feel threatened when there is the opportunity to be with their peers. They feel their own performance is being compared with others, and they fear that they might appear to be second best. All of this seems to indicate that competition blocks clergy communication and confidentiality.[3]

I have no doubt that this is true, because I have since seen it firsthand in the clergy I minister to. However, Brene Brown would suggest that there is a cost to hiding our problems and imperfections, and that is the loss of authenticity. At the heart of authenticity is the willingness to be vulnerable with others. She states, "Choosing authenticity means cultivating the courage to be imperfect . . . and to allow ourselves to be vulnerable."[4] In my own denomination, we formed a clergy wellness task force a few years ago to discuss

3. Gauger and Christie, *Clergy Stress*, 15.
4. Brown, *Gifts of Imperfection*, 50.

the many areas of wellness that needed to be addressed. Part of our goal was to create a help-seeking culture in which pastors would feel comfortable in sharing their struggles and the ways in which they had reached out for help and healing. One of the things we did was establish a monthly newsletter column in which clergy could share their experiences of challenge and how they have addressed them. In the past three years since its inception, we have heard from pastors who were experiencing family conflicts, suffered from anxiety or depression, admitted that they struggled with prayer, or shared how they handled problem situations in their churches, et cetera. One courageous soul even confessed her struggle with addiction and sought treatment with the support of her congregation.

Certainly, this level of opening oneself to the possible judgment of others is frightening and should be done with prayer and discernment, but the benefits of vulnerability often outweigh the cost. The courage to share your struggles can result in deeper connections with others as they identify with you and perhaps begin to believe that it might be possible for them to expose their own problems to the light of day. Your disclosure might give them hope that they too might prevail over something that feels impossible.

Perhaps some of you are asking yourself, why take the chance? My response is this—because you need clergy colleagues to travel this road with you. Clergy colleagues may be the only people who truly understand the challenges of this calling. When your other friends and family don't fully grasp the problems you face, clergy friends get it. More often than not, they have been there and done that. Having trusted colleagues you can turn to in times of frustration, hurt, discouragement, joy, blessing, and hope can be a real blessing to you on this journey. But you have to summon the courage to be vulnerable, to take the leap of revealing your own fallibility. It's okay that you don't always know what to do in a particular situation. It's okay to make mistakes, because that's how we learn. It's okay to ask others for guidance or reassurance or just an understanding ear. Vulnerability is a key factor in this thing called clergy wellness.

So how does one begin to create connections with fellow clergy? Many denominations encourage pastors to participate in clergy clusters, groups of pastors who serve the churches in a particular geographic area. Some of these groups are helpful and healthy, while others, because of flawed leadership or that one member who is toxic—monopolizing conversation and failing to honor confidentiality—are less so. If that is the case, you might want to seek out other connections that feel safe to you. This may be a hand-picked group of pastors you know and trust, or an ecumenical ministry association, or a seminary cohort. Collegial groups can be either formal or informal. One young pastor discovered a deep bond with some of his seminary classmates after a course they all took together. Since then they have continued to be in regular contact with each other through texting, Facebook, and phone calls even though they live far apart from one another. This has been a life-giving cohort for him. Another pastor I know in a small town with many conservative evangelical churches found it helpful to connect with the other two pastors of mainline Protestant denominations in that community. They often met for coffee or lunch to share ideas, frustrations, and dreams for their churches. My sister, who was the first solo female pastor in her town, connected with two other female pastors who moved there over time, and they supported one another and planned many ecumenical events together.

Serving in a remote community does make it more difficult to maintain relationships with clergy colleagues, but this problem can be surmounted by the use of technology. Video conferencing, text messaging, e-mails, and phone calls can often be just as connectional as face-to-face meetings. Sometimes it is even easier to share deeply personal issues when you are using more indirect means of communication. Some of my deepest conversations with close friends have occurred via a messaging app.

Trust is a key factor in choosing the people you will be able to be vulnerable with. In my work as a mental-health counselor, I taught many of my clients how to develop trust in relationships. The first thing is to give it time. Let the relationship unfold without forcing it or expecting deep connection right off the bat. Observe the other person for signs that they are trustworthy or not. Do they share confidential information with you about others? (Not a good sign.) Do they engage in gossip? Are they addicted to drama and have poor boundaries? Or do they respect your boundaries and give you space without pressing for personal sharing too soon? Do they appear to be a person of integrity? Do they exhibit healthy boundaries themselves? If you do share something personal, do they respond appropriately and honor what you have shared? These are all good clues that someone is worthy of your trust and safe to be vulnerable with.

All of this may seem like hard work and perhaps more trouble than it's worth, but the benefits of having clergy colleagues you can share ministry with can be invaluable. People who truly understand and accept you for who you are can be a gift and a blessing on this path of ministry.

Marriage and Family

Of the three categories of relationship, family is the most important. These are the people who are going to be with you for the long haul, the ones who will be with you even after your career in ministry is over. Your family members are the ones who know you most intimately and have the best vantage point from which to observe your level of functioning and detect problems before they get too severe. However, in order for this to happen, the relationships need to be healthy, which requires time and attention. Nowhere is this more important than in the marriage relationship.

The statistics on clergy marriages are alarming. An article published by the Francis Schaeffer Institute of Church Leadership reports that 77 percent of clergy did not rate their marriages positively.[5] In addition, 38 percent of clergy in the survey were either divorced or in the process of divorcing. Another 30 percent reported either a one-time sexual encounter with a parishioner or an ongoing affair. Given that the rate of infidelity in the general population is between 10 and 20 percent, this is an alarming statistic. What are the contributing factors to this dismal state of marriage in the church?

For starters, clergy spouses are often frustrated by the unrealistic expectations the congregation has for their role in the church. Wives are expected to be active in women's organizations, play the role of gracious hostess, and/or lead Bible studies or other women's groups. Whether these activities fit the gifts she actually possesses is beside the point. In the meantime, some clergy husbands are expected to perform repairs to the parsonage and even the church, especially if the budget prohibits the hiring of professionals to do that work. In addition to these expectations, which are often based on the spouse of the previous pastor(s), spouses can grow to resent the time demands of the church that take away from family and couple time. Over time, they can come to believe that the church is more important to you than they are. One therapist has said that United Methodist clergy spouses are some of the angriest people he has ever counseled.[6]

And what of the clergy themselves? When things are not good at home, when quality time is not a priority, and interactions with one's spouse are often contentious, the pastor is vulnerable to seeking positive attention and affirmation elsewhere. And it's not hard to find. A warm

5. Gauger and Christie, *Clergy Stress*, 2.
6. Gauger and Christie, *Clergy Stress*, 18.

and caring pastor is often the object of parishioner "crushes." This is a phenomenon familiar to psychotherapists. Whether doing therapy or providing pastoral care, professionals often adopt a persona that is totally focused on the person in front of them. Their own issues are not a part of the conversation, and the patient/parishioner receives 100 percent of their compassionate attention. It's pretty easy to "fall in love" with someone who gives you that kind of unconditional positive regard. What clergy need to remember when this happens is that the parishioner is not infatuated with the real you, the one with flaws and foibles, the one who loses his or her temper at times, and isn't always as loving and kind as this person is experiencing you in the church setting.

I can only guess at the factors that led to my childhood pastor engaging in an extramarital affair, but the scenario I have just described is a strong possibility. However, this was not my only experience of a former pastor getting caught in an affair. A pastor of many years experience was serving a new church start, and a young woman who had recently joined the church expressed interest in entering the ministry. Our pastor began mentoring her as she discerned her call, and, since the church was renting space in a school for Sunday worship, they met in the pastor's home while his wife was at work. Inevitably, the intimacy of such a relationship and the privacy of their meeting place led to a sexual relationship. Ultimately, the affair was discovered, the pastor was fired, and his wife divorced him. Shame consumed him, and he was unable to find meaningful work in ministry for several years.

These stories and more point to the importance of prevention. First of all, be alert to feelings of attraction to someone that is not your spouse. To a certain degree, this is normal, as long as the feelings are not hidden away like some guilty secret. However, be alert to when the mild attraction becomes more than that. If you find yourself fantasizing or flirting, you need to ask yourself what that is about. Are there troubles at home, a lack of communication or affection? If that is the case, perhaps your feelings are a symptom of a troubled marriage. If so, remind yourself that in the same way that a congregant never gets a full picture of who you are, neither do you get a full picture of them. They are going to be painting themselves in as positive a light as possible for their pastor. Acknowledgement of what is happening usually causes the attraction to lose some of its power. However, recognition of the dynamics at play is not enough. Then it is time to act to resolve the issues close to home rather than acting on the attraction.

Often, affairs, whether emotional or sexual, begin with a lowering of boundaries. If you notice that you are sharing more personal information with someone than you normally would, consider this an alarm bell going off in your head. At the same time that this opening of a door is happening, there is the closing of a door between you and your spouse. You may find yourself shutting down, sharing less, or turning away from intimacy. And once the door to the other is open to emotional intimacy, physical intimacy is not far behind. Before that happens, it is important to reverse the direction of sharing from this person to whom you are attracted and direct it back toward your spouse.

Begin to truly work on your marriage. This means scheduling quality time, both with and without children. It means date nights, lunch dates (even if that means peanut butter sandwiches in the park), pillow talk, play activities (see chapter 9), or pretty much anything that enhances emotional and physical intimacy. It means occasional overnight getaways. But if I were to name the single most important factor in keeping a marriage vital, it would be *communication*. Talk to each other! When things are hard, hash it out. When talking leads to fighting, seek marital counseling. When it feels like there's an abyss between you, reach out. Find something that unites you. Rekindle the fun of earlier times. Talk about your pain, not just what the other is doing that drives you crazy. And talk about your work.

One former client was feeling distant from his wife, stating that they didn't talk anymore. When I asked if he talked to her about his work, he said he tried not to, feeling that she wasn't interested or that she wouldn't want to be burdened with his problems. I challenged him on this, suggesting that most spouses are pretty sensitive to mood, and when you're upset, they will spend a lot of time wondering why and imagining things that aren't true. When a spouse goes silent, their partner's first thought will often be "Have I done something wrong to cause this?" They feel shut out, and they in turn might start to shut down. Of course, there will be times when you just don't feel like talking, and that's perfectly okay. There is more to communication than talking. Perhaps you can develop a system of signals that tell your spouse what kind of day it was, what mood you're in, and whether or not you need time to decompress before being bombarded with the kids' needs or your spouse's desire to tell you about his or her day. Create a chart with "emoticons" you can point to, or a number system that rates your day, or even a hand signal that indicates how many minutes you need to wind down before you feel human again. But always come back to the personal sharing that keeps relationships strong and healthy. The benefits of a good marriage are manifold for both the clergy person and their spouse. Many studies support the idea that people with a positive marital relationship are both physically and mentally healthier than their unmarried or unhappily married counterparts. Thus, marital health is an essential part of clergy wellness.

Now, let's talk about the kids. Spending quality time with your children is a challenge for every working parent in our hectic and complex world. At the moment our children enter our lives, a guilt button is installed that gets pushed whenever we feel that we aren't living up to our own expectations of what it means to be a good parent. We wonder if we're giving them enough of our time and attention, enough praise to counteract the corrections or criticisms, enough enrichment experiences, enough hugs, enough of everything we hope to be able to pass on to our kids. No parent is spared the guilt that comes when we have to make hard choices between two equally valued commitments. Clergy often have to decide which is more important—the church board meeting about a vital issue in the life of the church, or your child's piano recital. On any given day, the choice could go either way. Perhaps we would do well to adopt the "possession arrow" rule from college basketball, where the teams take turns getting possession of the ball when it goes out of bounds. Some days the decision is made in favor of the church, and some days the family takes precedence.

In a survey of people who work for the common good, mostly in non-profits devoted to fighting racism, poverty, homelessness, domestic violence, et cetera, they found that most of those who were parents were highly concerned about the cost to their children due to the demanding work they did. Yet the researchers saw "little evidence that the people [they] interviewed spent less time with their children than most hard-working parents."[7] In fact, they found that those parents were quite thoughtful about explaining their absences in terms of their commitment to the common good and felt that the children understood and appreciated the importance of their work.

Perhaps clergy parents can be reassured by this anecdotal evidence and take a page from the "play book" of mothers and fathers who share a similar vocation and concern for their relationship with their children. For example, while the schedule of clergy life defies established family routines, the patchwork calendar of church activities may also allow clergy to attend school

7. Parks et al., *Common Fire*, 174.

activities that "eight-to-five" parents might not be able to. A clergy parent might have the ability to chaperone a child's field trip if it falls on a day with no meetings or hospital visits. They might be able to attend a special party or parent/child breakfast or lunch at school or a concert or sporting event that is scheduled during the typical work day of other parents.

Even when you are able to schedule family time or attend your kids' school activities, it is also important that every one of your children gets one-on-one time with you on occasion. Try clearing time for a "date" with each of your kids periodically, even if it's only once every three or four months. Take them out to lunch or dinner or to the park or the zoo. The details of when and where and for how long are of little importance. What matters is that being the sole focus of your love and attention makes your child feel that they matter to you and that they are special.

Taking your child to work with you on occasion is another possibility when the requirements of your day don't preclude it. One pastor mom I know has incorporated her children into many aspects of her ministry. When the church engages in mission projects such as food drives or meals for the homeless, her kids are there helping. When the church is hosting a community event, the children are making posters to advertise it. Even on Sunday mornings, her children often join her up front, sometimes reading parts of the liturgy, sometimes copying their mother's gestures during communion, other times just sitting near her as she leads worship. Another clergy mother took a two-minute "recess" in the middle of worship when her daughter became distraught over a small scratch and needed her mother to put on the bandage even though her father was sitting right there! When children are this steeped in the life of the church, there is no sense of their parent's work as being something separate from them. However, this isn't necessarily the appropriate approach for every clergy family. Each family must be prayerful and intentional about what is best for their children.

A retired pastor I see for spiritual direction shared this story about her own children. By the time this woman received her first call to a church, her daughter was just starting college and did not move with the family to their new home. Donna stated that this was probably a good thing, as the daughter was fairly introverted and would have been uncomfortable with the attention she would have received as the pastor's daughter. On the other hand, her son, who was in high school at the time, was just the opposite. He had a wonderful high school experience in their new community. He helped to start a youth group in the church and was very active in that ministry.

However, when his school invited local pastors to come and connect with students during lunch hour, he asked his mother not to attend. He felt that the confusion of parent and pastor roles would have been uncomfortable for him, so Donna agreed not to participate.

This story illustrates the need to know your children well and honor their desires for the amount of engagement they are comfortable with in the church. The same is true of your spouse. It can sometimes be hard to hold those boundaries with a congregation eager to embrace the pastor's family and involve them in the life of the church. And as we've already discussed, there are those parishes whose expectations run high for the role of the spouse and children due to former clergy family members who were beloved and highly regarded. It is important that you insist your family be given the space to decide for themselves how much or how little they want to be a part of the life of the congregation. Give your spouse and children opportunities to share their feelings and desires with you in an atmosphere of safety and acceptance. Be alert to your own hopes and dreams for what it might look like to be a clergy family, and be willing to let go of those expectations so that you can allow the gift of who they really are to bless your family and your ministry.

Additionally, spending time together as a family is an important respite for everyone. This makes vacation a vital ingredient in cultivating positive relationships and happy memories for the whole family. Many pastors are guilty of not taking all of the vacation time they are allowed. It's hard to get away, hard to find a time when the church calendar and the family members' calendars are not in conflict. And invariably, someone in the church is going to die while you are away. A clergy couple that I worked with many years ago was convinced that their vacations were cursed. It seemed like *every time* they planned a getaway, there would be a death or serious illness or accident in the congregation that would require them to cut short or cancel their plans.

There is an apocryphal story about a pastor who was getting ready to leave on vacation. He was going over all the things that would need to be taken care of in his absence with the administrative assistant and the chair of the church council, but they were still anxious. "Give us a number where we can get in touch with you in case of an emergency." (Clearly this was prior to the advent of the cell phone.) The pastor was reluctant, but the two church officials insisted. Finally, he wrote a number on a piece of paper, folded it in half, put it in an envelope, sealed it and handed it to the council chair. On the outside of the envelope, it read "To be opened ONLY in case of emergency." The pastor left on his vacation, and sure enough, a few days later, an emergency came up, and the two who had been left in charge felt compelled to open the envelope. Imagine their surprise when they saw what their pastor had written—911!

Obviously, this would not work in real life. However, it does speak to the need to educate your church leaders and staff about the importance of a pastor's self-care and the definition of an emergency. As mentioned in chapter 5, it's helpful to be explicit about what constitutes an emergency. It also helps to have a contingency plan in place, which may mean identifying a parishioner or fellow pastor who can respond to emergencies that require pastoral care. If there is someone who is terminally ill, let that family know you will be gone and will not be able to conduct a memorial service until after you return if their family member passes during that time. Obviously, you cannot plan for every contingency, but you can identify the possible situations that might arise in your absence and devise a course of action that will allow you to continue with your vacation without guilt.

Sometimes, it's not the staff-parish committee that needs to be reminded of the importance of self-care but the pastor. You and your family need this extended time to relax and unwind, to enjoy each other, to be reminded of why you love each other, and to have fun! If you can't remember the benefits of vacation, it's been too long. So take all the vacation days your contract specifies. Don't leave anything on the table. If there is an emergency that disrupts your vacation and absolutely necessitates an early return, keep track of the days you missed out on and use them as comp time at a later date.

Another complication of planning time away is the expense. Vacations aren't cheap, and a pastor's salary doesn't always stretch that far. However, there are some options if you can't afford anything fancy. Many church camps offer pastors and their families a few free nights at camp during the off-season. Or if you ask around, you may discover that some of your parishioners own vacation homes they might let you use for a few days. Don't hesitate to take advantage of these offers. I know one clergy family that spends their allotted three days at a church camp every year, and that vacation is the source of many of their fondest memories. They play together, romp the woods and hills surrounding the camp, and sit by the fireside talking and telling stories every night. It is a wonderful bonding experience that they return to again and again. In addition, now that the kids are older, they spend their summers at the same camp on staff as counselors.

Reflection Questions

1. How often do you spend time with friends? Does that feel like enough? If not, what are some ways you can increase the frequency of your contact with them?

2. What are the blessings you receive from those relationships?

3. Do you have supportive relationships with your fellow clergy? If not, what are the barriers to that? Are these barriers real or perceived?

4. Have you ever felt an attraction to someone in your congregation? If so, what factors contributed to that?

5. What is the quality of your marriage or committed relationship? What areas need improvement?

6. If you have children, what is the quality of those relationships?

7. What would your children say are the pros and cons of being a "preacher's kid"?

8. What is one thing you can do with your children to enrich your relationships with them?

9

Sacred Play

Finding Balance for the Holy Work of Ministry

So I recommend having fun, because there is nothing better for people to do in this world than to eat, drink, and enjoy life. That way they will experience some happiness along with all the hard work God gives them.

—ECCLESIASTES 8:15 (NLT)

Why Play?

When was the last time you carved out time in your schedule for play? It seems rather inconsequential, doesn't it, in the midst of the weighty work of ministry? Such a silly, childish thing to do! And yet, aren't there times when you see children playing and long for those carefree times of long ago? I often lead a retreat I developed on Sacred Play, and I love listening to the stories that participants tell about their favorite childhood play activities. You can see their faces light up with pleasure as they recall those happy times. And as they share, they begin to see how closely their childhood play is related to the person they've become as an adult.

Trevor Hudson, a South African pastor who has written numerous books on spirituality, once gave a plenary address at a conference I was attending. He is a very tall and lanky man, and he was telling us how much he loved Superman as a boy. He was especially enamored of the big red S that was emblazoned on the front of Superman's hero outfit, broad chest emphasizing his power and strength. "I would have loved to have an outfit like that," he said, "but all I could have managed on my skinny chest was an italicized I!" Of course, this got a big laugh as the audience pictured this gangly kid trying to imagine himself as Superman.

I imagine many of you played super-hero as a kid. Most of us have. And now, in one aspect, you *are* superheroes. The life of clergy is the life of a spiritual superhero—saving souls, nurturing your congregations, and marshalling the church to battle evil of a different sort, things like war, hunger, poverty, injustice, and oppression. But this superhero life takes a huge toll. The people you serve have such unrealistic expectations for you. You must be able to do it all, whether it takes forty, sixty, or eighty hours a week, smiling all the while, showering blessings on all you meet, never getting angry, and never complaining, even when your dinner hour is interrupted yet again because someone forgot to lock the church door, buy elements for communion, or send out reminders for the next ad council meeting. It's just part of the job. The problem is that it is rarely fun anymore, and it certainly isn't play! This is a life without balance, and for some, burn-out or even breakdown is just around the corner.

In Ecclesiastes, Solomon states that there is "a season for every activity under heaven."[1] He goes on to list several pairs of opposites—a time to be born and a time to die, a time for planting and a time for uprooting, a time for mourning and a time for dancing, et cetera. The implied suggestion is that balance is achieved through opposites, from which we might infer that there is a time for sacred work and a time for sacred play. What if, when Jesus urged us to become like little children in order to enter the kingdom of God, he was referring to more than their natural faith, trust, and innocence? Maybe he was also talking about their playfulness and exuberance for life.

I think we often forget that Jesus was once a child himself. Perhaps this is because the Bible gives only a cursory glimpse of his childhood. In only two of the Gospels does Jesus make an appearance as a baby, and even then he is depicted as an angelic infant with a halo over his head. We don't hear him cry or see him crawl. We don't know if he was ever up to mischief. By contrast, in the Hindu religion, Krishna is a child god who is nicknamed the "butter thief," because he gets into the pot of freshly churned butter and makes mischief. His mother scolds him affectionately, revealing a vision of loving and endless tolerance that reminds us of the unconditional love and forgiveness of God. Diana Eck, in her book *Encountering God*, describes a delightful worship service she attended in India in which toys were offered

1. Eccl 3:1.

to the child god Krishna by elderly priests who played with these toys at the altar. She remarked, "I was startled—dumbfounded really—at the notion that one might worship the Lord by offering the gift of play."[2]

The problem is that there are so many things that get in the way of play, not the least of which are our crowded day planners. A favorite Calvin and Hobbes cartoon shows the pair up in a tree idling away the hours. Calvin looks down from his perch and ponders, "Ever notice how people always try to do two things at once? They talk on the phone while they drive. They watch TV while they eat. They listen to music while they work. People never focus on any one thing to enjoy it or do it well. *We* focus on doing nothing at all." A dozing Hobbes quips, "You're breaking my concentration."[3] The problem is that in this cultured adult world we occupy, play can seem frivolous, immature, and a waste of time. What will people think if they see us rolling around in the grass or playing hide and seek or being spontaneously silly? And what will *you* think? When we begin to consider the idea of play, we come smack up against our inhibitions, our self-talk, and often our upbringing. What were the messages we got as a child about work and play? How has that shaped your approach to the idea of having fun in your daily life?

Our culture also shapes our beliefs about play to an alarming degree. Margaret Guenther, in her book *Holy Listening,* says, "Our culture has made *leisure* an industry, but knows very little about *play*. Often what we call 'play' is competitive or compulsive, because the aesthetic dimension of true play, its holy uselessness, goes against our grain."[4] We are a society that worships productivity, usefulness, and competence, a culture that has tunnel vision that is only focused on the end game, the product of our work. When we are working, we can shove aside our self-doubt and convince ourselves that we have value, that we are worthy, but we forget that works righteousness is not the kind of faith God wants from us. So what does this term "holy uselessness" mean? I think that it is only when we stop and play that we become aware of how much God delights in us, how much our Creator longs to run on the beach with us, or play catch, or watch butterflies, or swing from the branches of a tree with us. We discover that God loves us for who we are, not for what we do. Play liberates us from the confines of our own perfectionism, from our need to acquire and achieve, and from

2. Eck, *Encountering God,* 105.

3. See Watterson, "Calvin & Hobbes," 24.

4. Guenther, *Holy Listening,* 58.

our anxieties about tomorrow, for play is utterly lived in the moment. Play allows us to become more fully who we are. We can shed our masks during play and allow ourselves to be known to others and to God.

For those of you who are not fully on board with me yet, let me expound on a few of the tangible benefits of play. In addition to what I believe are the spiritual benefits of play, there are some practical elements to be considered as well.

- Anti-aging: Play may be the true fountain of youth. My father was an avid outdoorsman, snow skiing, golfing, and even sky-diving into his 90s. There's an old adage that states, "We don't stop playing because we grow old, we grow old because we stop playing!"

- Physical fitness: Many play activities require you to be physically active. Since clergy find that their busy schedules are anathema to a healthy diet or regular exercise, play can be more motivating than spending an hour at the gym every day.

- Stress reduction: When you have the opportunity to get your mind off your worries and the demands of your ministry through play, this will go a long way toward reducing your stress. Laughter produces endorphins and shuts down the excessive production of the stress hormone cortisol. This also boosts your immune system, which is often compromised when you work too hard and fail to get enough rest.

- Better sleep: When you can set aside the intrusive thoughts about your to-do list or a problematic situation in your church and immerse yourself in a fun activity, you will likely find that you sleep better. Physical play also helps tire out your body. Sometimes, when we are too sedentary, sleep doesn't come easily, but throwing yourself into a backyard game of football or capture the flag can make for a better night's sleep. (Just don't do this right before bedtime!)

- Mental fitness: Doing word puzzles or playing word games are important for keeping our minds active, especially as we age. These activities are proven to help prevent or postpone the onset of Alzheimer's and other types of dementia. While it was once thought that our brains could not grow new cells after a certain age, new research is beginning to challenge that. There is also evidence that new neural pathways can be developed through certain mental activities beyond what was previously thought.

- Building community and family bonding: We've all heard the old adage, the family that prays together, stays together. I think it also holds true if you switch pray to play. There is something about engaging in family recreational activities that enhances relationships and creates happy memories that can be recalled for years to come. Laughing together creates a lasting bond. This is also true for adult friendships. It is often difficult for clergy to maintain friendships due to conflicting schedules, often settling for a quick lunch where all you have time for is a quick catch-up on life events. Whereas, play can help create deeper, long-lasting bonds over shared enjoyment and the camaraderie of sport.

What Is Play?

Several years ago, the devotional magazine *Alive Now* published an issue on play. On the inside of the front cover was this quote: "Play is the exuberant expression of our being. It is at the heart of our creativity, our sexuality, and our most carefree moments of devotion. It helps us live with absurdity, paradox, and mystery. It feeds our joy and wonder. It keeps our search for meaning down to earth."[5]

When I first began researching play, I decided that a park bench next to a playground would be the best place to start. I found a good park where lots of children were running, swinging, climbing, and otherwise having a great time and sat down to watch the fun. I observed the children for at least an hour, reveling in their revelry. Their squeals and laughter were a tonic for my soul and caused me to ponder what their play was all about. Soon I was journaling furiously as questions turned into insight through a free-flowing stream of consciousness. Here is part of what I wrote that day:

> Why do children play? To revel in their bodies and the things it can do, to challenge themselves, test their limits, and learn new skills (although I doubt they would call it that). To exult in the sensations of spinning, sliding, and swinging—that stomach-churning gravity drop that happens when you swing higher than the chains can keep up. We called that "sugar bumps" when I was a kid. Play is about doing something scary, trusting oneself to the universe and letting go. Play is the fun way to face your fears! (At this point, one child was chasing another, roaring like a monster, while the

5. From the Play practice homepage at www.SpiritualityandPractice.com.

one being chased shrieked with delight.) Play is imagination, the creative energy that allows you to be anything, try anything, travel the world without leaving your back yard, or explore the jungles of Africa from the confines of the park down the street. This kind of play erases limitations so that you can discover who you really are. I know a lot of grown-ups who could really use some of this kind of play in their lives. Too bad that adult responsibility has smothered and stifled our childhood instinct for play. How dull and boring we adults have become! Come to think of it, play is healing, too. Remember how you used to fight with your best friend and want to play with him or her again ten minutes later? Maybe we could turn our world leaders loose on the playground and see what happens. Maybe they'd learn to cooperate and take turns. Maybe an occasional tumble and a healthy dose of laughter would teach them to lighten up just a little. They say that music is the universal language, and that's probably true. But I think play might come in a close second. Put a bunch of kids without a shared language in a room full of toys, or turn them loose on a playground, and I'm pretty sure they would be able to figure it out.

Another good resource for me was the body of literature on play therapy. I was a play therapist myself at one time and learned a great deal from the work of Garry Landreth, a giant in the field and a kind, gentle man who reminds me of Fred Rogers. In his many books and workshops, he teaches that true play has five distinct characteristics:[6]

- Play is *pleasurable*. I'm quite sure that none of us would engage in play if it didn't give us pleasure. This also speaks to the understanding that not everyone enjoys the same play activities. Some people don't enjoy playing card games, for instance, and no matter how much we might try to convince them that they will really enjoy the game, it will never feel like play to them. Pleasure is the essence of play.

- Play is *intrinsically complete*. That is, it is satisfying in and of itself, not dependent on any kind of external reward. In other words, you don't have to be rewarded with a lollipop in order to be willing to engage in play. Children and adults play just for the sake of the play.

- Play is *connectional*. Relationships are often built and strengthened through play. There is a bond that develops through mutual play and enjoyment. This doesn't necessarily mean that all play requires having

6. Landreth, *Play Therapy*, 60–62.

playmates. I'm sure many of you can recall playing alone as a child, building with blocks or Legos, playing school or house with dolls or stuffed animals, riding your bicycle, climbing trees, et cetera. These may have been the times when you were connecting with true self, with creation, and even with the Divine. Playmates are a wonderful, but not required, aspect of play.

- Play is *focused on meaning, not purpose*. Play needs no purpose. It just is. This goes back to the idea of holy uselessness in which we let go of our need to achieve and produce. We are not playing in order to accomplish something or get somewhere. Play is about the art of being, which gives us meaning.

- Play is *freeing rather than restrictive*. True play doesn't have a lot of rules. Play should be more yes than no, more do than don't. We want to expand our world through play rather than make it so narrow that we are unable to truly express ourselves.

Perhaps a story told by a clergy participant at one of my retreats will help to illustrate these five points better than I ever could. This clergy person, we'll call him Joe, was working many years ago for a wilderness program for troubled youth who had a history of juvenile incarceration. The counselors and kids had been back-packing in British Columbia for several days and had returned to base camp for the ferry ride back to civilization the next morning. The base camp was located on a remote inlet that is world-renowned for its natural beauty. That evening after dark, the group walked down to the dock to gaze at the stars. It was a moonless night, so the Milky Way was visible in all its splendor.

At some point, one of the boys leaned over to look at the water lapping against the side of the dock, and something fell out of his pocket. There was a splash and then a surprising burst of light in the water. The darkness of the night sky had created the perfect condition for the phosphorescence in the sea water to be revealed. Everyone got very excited by this natural light show, so they began swirling their hands in the water to make patterns of light, and then someone threw in a rock. This created a small explosion of light, and then the magic began in earnest. The rock disturbed fish that had been swimming near the dock and caused them to dart away, creating arrows of phosphorescent green in the murky darkness. Again and again, they threw rocks and watched the brilliant bursts, followed by the streaks of light. And then someone said the inevitable words, "I'm gonna jump in!"

Imagine a cannonball that explodes into a brilliant eruption of light. Soon, all of the youth and their counselors were jumping into the water with abandon, reveling in this mystical light show. That's when the seals joined in the fun. Attracted by all the commotion, the curious seals came to see what the fuss was about, their phosphorescent outlines looking like torpedoes racing through the sea-green water. The group jumped and swam with the seals until they were winded and wobbly, collapsing on the pier to catch their breath. Then someone said, "Let's do that again," and off they went. Joe doesn't remember how long this went on, for it was a time out of time. But even years later, he uses words like magical, joyous, transcendent, and sacramental to describe this moment of true play. And he is grateful for the gift he was given on a dark night in a time and place far away from the workaday world where he could discover the magic, the communion, and the blessing of play.

Now that we have a sense of what play is, I want to turn our attention to two things play definitely is not. Play is not virtual. Play is firmly grounded in the real, so video games and television would not be considered play. I have certainly had some pushback over the years on this topic, especially as the popularity of video games has ballooned to the level of obsession among youth and young adults. But if you look at the five criteria for play, probably the only one that video games meets is that it is pleasurable. The problem is that many adults who play video games do it to numb out. That's okay—we all need that escape from reality from time to time—as long as you don't consider it a substitute for the restorative benefits of play.

The same is true of watching television. Perhaps our friends Calvin and Hobbes can help illustrate this point. As Calvin turns on the television, he begins to describe his "method" for watching. He says, "I try to make television-watching a complete forfeiture of experience. Notice how I keep my jaw slack, so my mouth hangs open. I try not to swallow either, so I drool, and I keep my eyes half-focused, so I don't use any muscles at all. I take a passive entertainment and extend the passivity to my entire being. I wallow in my lack of participation and response. I'm utterly inert." And then we see Hobbes walking away, muttering, "I'm going to leave before you start attracting flies."[7] Christine Valters Paintner writes, "There isn't anything wrong with watching TV or movies, but it is not the renewing of our souls, and when we use it to numb out rather than really replenish, it

---

7. Watterson, *Days Are Just Packed*, 20.

becomes a problem. We wonder why we are so drained all the time."[8] True play engages, renews, and replenishes.

There is also some tension around whether competitive games or sports could be considered play. In his book *Sacred Necessities,* Terry Hershey shares a "parable" about the playground of Eden, where there weren't just two people, but lots of people having fun together until a snake came along to suggest that in order for the play to be more meaningful, they should start keeping score.[9] Everybody thought this was a great idea, but it changed the nature of the play until eventually, they only played for an hour a day and spent the rest of the day fighting over the rules. When God found out what they were doing, he kicked them all out of the playground, because the garden was meant to be fun, and they clearly weren't having fun anymore. The problem is that scores have no meaning, and if you are playing to win, then you are not reaping the spiritual benefits of play. Even Calvin figured this out when he beat Hobbes at checkers. For three panels, he exults in his victory, declaring himself champion of the world and jumping up and down. Then in the final panel, he drops his arms to his side and says, "Is this all there is?"[10] Certainly, I have seen a group of close friends playing hoops on the basketball court and having great fun, connecting with their companions, enjoying their bodies, laughing, and being silly. I have also seen pick-up games that were fiercely competitive and intense, where play and fun were entirely absent. Perhaps it is a matter of balance. Competition can be friendly and fun, but it fails to be playful when it is only about winning or keeping score.

Types of Play

Returning to my observations of children on the playground, I began to see some distinct categories of play emerging. Combined with my own experiences of play, first in childhood and then as an adult, I came up with four different types of play with fairly fluid boundaries that allow for overlap. The first of these is body play. This would include running, jumping, climbing, swinging, playing catch, four-square, jump rope, sports, and even dancing. Remember David dancing as he brought the ark into Jerusalem as I mentioned in chapter 6. These types of activities are an expression of

8. Paintner, *Eyes of the Heart,* 4.

9. Hershey, *Sacred Necessities,* 130–32.

10. Watterson, *Days Are Just Packed,* 34.

spiritual joy, an exuberant celebration of what our bodies can do. They also bring us into community with others. When I ask adults about their favorite childhood play activities, frequently their responses include body play, such as riding bicycles, climbing trees, swimming at the local swimming hole, et cetera. These kinds of universal play activities get stored in our body memory and can be a touchstone for us as we age. There's truth to the saying that you never forget how to ride a bike.

When my mother was in a nursing care facility with dementia, my dad and I went to visit her on her birthday. I had brought some balloons, and she squealed in delight when she saw their bright colors. She immediately started batting at them with childish glee. It seemed that the balloons had awakened something primal in her, something that couldn't be quelled by the dementia. I asked her what color the balloons were, and even though she was wrong most of the time, nevertheless her responses were color words. Then I noticed that the facility had provided a "goodie bag" for her birthday, and in it was a bottle of soap bubbles. Smiling, I unscrewed the cap and pulled out the wand, slimy soap dripping down my fingers. Mother watched intently as luminescent bubbles flew from the plastic circle and floated over her bed. Body memory again conquered the prison of her mind as she swatted at the bubbles and popped the glistening orbs. This is the joy and the lasting impact of body play.

The second type of play, and perhaps the one that we engage in most easily as adults, is word play—jokes, puns, metaphors, and playful teasing. Poets like e. e. cummings excel at this kind of play. Certainly, we know that Jesus often used plays on words to illustrate important concepts in a way that listeners could identify with. Even prayer can be playful. Consider the proximity between play and pray. I think God appreciates whimsy as much as humans do. Even the nameless author of *The Cloud of Unknowing* suggests that playful prayer can be helpful in breaking through the internal barriers that keep you from experiencing God's presence in prayer. Donald Shockley, in his book *Private Prayers in Public Places*, states, "Human beings are born to laugh or at least to smile. Since humor is a gift from God, it is sometimes permissible to be playful when we are prayerful."[11]

As a writer and an inveterate journaler, there are times when I am waylaid by whimsy, and my writing takes off on flights of fancy. One such occurrence took place when I was outdoors enjoying a lovely spring day from an inviting expanse of lawn and noticed the moon plainly visible in

11. Shockley, *Private Prayers*, 12.

broad daylight. This inspired a journal entry that started like this: "The moon winked at me today. There I was, minding my own business, meditating on the beautiful blue sky from my patch of grass, when my vision was interrupted by a wispy semi-circle of white. 'What are you doing here?' I asked in astonishment." What followed was a silly conversation with the moon that ended with, "I smiled at the moon, who had also escaped from the ordinary, and winked back."

One of the exercises I typically ask retreat participants to do is to take a few minutes to play with words on paper and not be afraid to be silly. Despite the fact that adults often resist doing anything that might be considered silly, my clergy folk always seem to engage in this word play with enthusiasm. As I watch them during this activity, I often witness them scribbling away with grins on their faces. I wonder if their sense of abandon is the belief that word play is the most socially acceptable form of adult play. Regardless, word play is certainly the easiest to fit into the craziness of clergy life and allows us to incorporate fun into the workplace.

One of my most vivid memories of childhood play is of turning my tricycle upside down and pretending the large front wheel was the helm of a pirate ship. Games of make believe and "Let's pretend" belong to the category of imaginative play. This might also include an afternoon of watching clouds and finding rabbits, dragons, and ducks in the sky. Day-dreaming, creative writing, reading, music, visual arts, and even coloring can be considered imaginative play. Calvin's alter ego Spaceman Spiff allows him to explore other worlds from a perch in his backyard tree house. When we use our imaginations, we come closer to God. Imagination was the beginning of all that exists. God's imagination resulted in the weaving of creation, and whenever we engage in imaginative play, we are participating in the ongoing act of creation, co-creating with God a dream of what could be. Playful imagining is a good way for clergy to disengage themselves from the rut of traditional ideas and old ways of doing things.

When I give clergy an everyday object and ask them to come up with as many alternative uses for it as they can, hilarity ensues. An umbrella becomes a boat, a soup pot becomes a helmet or a drum, and a dust mop becomes a wig or a dancing partner or . . . . The list is endless. And fun. I imagine that God is smiling when we do this.

The last type of play is earth play. I love the passage in Proverbs that speaks about Wisdom participating in the act of creation. "The LORD created me [Wisdom] when God's purpose first unfolded, before the oldest of

God's works. From everlasting I was firmly set, from the beginning, before earth came into being. . . . I was by God's side, a master crafter, delighting God day by day, ever at play in God's presence, at play everywhere in the world."[12] I don't think it is coincidence that one of the synonyms for play is recreation. When we play in creation, we are participating in a re-creation of the world and of ourselves. We are rediscovering and reconnecting with the delights of Eden and the fellowship with God that Adam and Eve enjoyed there. Playing in nature restores us to ourselves. Ultimately, it allows us to disconnect from the modern world for a while and set aside the worries and cares of the church while we revel in God's handiwork and receive God's abundance and delight. This change of scenery is vital to the balance we seek through sacred play.

Earth play can include making mud pies, building sand castles, hiking, climbing trees, rolling in the grass, chasing butterflies, looking at the stars, running through the waves as they ebb and flow along the ocean shore. Calvin is the absolute expert on earth play. One comic strip shows him digging a hole in the dirt, adding water, and jumping in. At the end of the day, as he enters the house caked in mud and is met by his chagrined mother, he says simply, "It couldn't be avoided."[13] Another depicts him shedding his clothes at bath time and examining his filthy body. "Wow, look at the grass stains on my skin," he remarks, "I say, if your knees aren't green by the end of the day, you ought to seriously re-examine your life."[14] Calvin speaks truth. Earth play grounds us in God's goodness and opens our eyes to holy moments. This is so perfectly illustrated by Joe's experience of the sacrament of swimming in the dark and playing with the light. Earth play allows us to discover the divine everywhere, for creation reveals the very nature of God. Every created thing bears the DNA of God and will speak to us of the divine nature if we but listen. The psalmist writes, "The heavens are telling of the glory of God; and their expanse is declaring the work of His hands."[15]

Conditions for Play

Perhaps the thing that takes the most imagination is how you begin to incorporate more play into your life. Making your work more playful is

12. Prov 8:22–23, 30–31a (JB)/
13. Watterson, *Days Are Just Packed*, 38.
14. Watterson, *Days Are Just Packed*, 116.
15. Ps 19:1 (NAS).

a good start, but it can't end there. Play is absolutely necessary as a counterpoint to the intensity of clergy life. Walking with people through some of the most difficult times in their lives and trying to be a worthy prophet of God's kingdom can be a heavy burden, one that needs release through the healing act of play. Clergy need to be able to "let off steam" in healthy ways, and laughter is one of the best ways I know. But it is easy to feel guilty for taking time to play when others are struggling or when the pile of work on your desk is over-flowing. That's why the most essential condition for sacred play is permission. I'm not suggesting you seek out permission from your staff-parish committee or your congregation or even your family. The hardest person to get permission from is you! However, practice makes perfect, so just make a start, and it will get easier as you go along.

Another essential ingredient is intention. Be purposeful. Sit down with your calendar and begin to block out times for play. At first, it might just be fifteen minutes, but as you look farther out on the calendar, some larger chunks of time will open up for you. My experience has been that if you take the time for play, you will become more efficient and effective when you are working, which then makes more room for fun.

Other conditions under which the possibility for play flourishes are spontaneity, flexibility, variety, creativity, and daring. Many of people's favorite memories of play began spontaneously, developing naturally out of a situation they were in at the moment, when they were able to flow with it and let go of inhibitions. Again, Joe's story is a perfect example. Rigid agendas don't often have room for fun in them. Let go of preconceived notions of when or how an opportunity for play will unfold. Use your creativity to see what is possible. Dare to be silly or do something you think you're not good at or that seems childish. Mix it up. Don't do the same thing every time you engage in play. Remember that variety is the spice of life. Open yourself up to the potential for play to become a sacred experience, one in which you are refreshed and renewed in the enjoyment of all the gifts of a playful God. Michael Yaconelli relates a story about a time when he came upon his son and some friends who were jumping on the bed.[16] Yaconelli lost his temper and told the boys to stop it immediately. Later, regretting his outburst, he wondered what Jesus would have done in that situation. Immediately he had a vision of Jesus, joyously jumping on the bed.

16. Yaconelli, *Dangerous Wonder*, 73.

Reflection Questions

1. What were your favorite play activities as a child? Do they connect in some way with who you are today?

2. What are your internal barriers to play? What are your internalized messages from childhood about play?

3. What does "holy uselessness" mean to you? Why is it important?

4. Reflect on a memory of play that profoundly impacted you. What were the elements of play that were present?

5. What are your current go-to play activities? What benefits do you gain from them?

10

Prophetic Narratives

Renewing Your Sense of Call

God said, ". . . I will remember my covenant that is between me and you and every living creature . . . ."

—GENESIS 9:15

Remembering and Forgetting

This chapter is about remembering. It is about remembering your call and all the ways in which God was faithful to the covenant God made with you as you answered this call. It is about remembering the ways that God equipped, empowered, and sustained you as you lived out that call. One of the best ways to do this is by revisiting the prophetic narratives in the Hebrew scriptures and engaging deeply in the stories, placing your own stories alongside them, and seeing the ways in which God has been steadfastly present in your ministry. It is through remembering the mighty and gracious acts of God that you are re-energized to do the work of God for the people of God. But first, let's talk for a moment about this idea of remembering. Bringing back memories can be a tricky business. Some of our memories aren't so pleasant, are they? In order to resolve this tension between positive and negative memories, let's take a look at two significant passages in the book of Isaiah.

In Isaiah 46:9, it says, "Remember the former things of old; for I am God, and there is no other; I am God, and there is no one like me . . . ," but in Isaiah 43:18–19a, the prophet writes, "Do *not* remember the former things, or consider the things of old. I am about to do a new thing; now it springs forth, do you not perceive it?" (emphasis mine). Within the space of three chapters, Isaiah first tells us "do *not* remember the former things" and then "*do* remember the former things." It's a bit confusing, isn't it? If we are to believe anything other than that Isaiah was confused, we must find a way to resolve the dialectic created by these two opposing passages.

There is strong support for the passage in Isaiah 46 calling God's people to remember. Much of Hebrew scripture is focused on remembrance—remembering God's covenant, God's saving miracles, God's mercy and lovingkindness. The prophets often admonished the Israelites to remember who they were as a nation and to remember God's law. Much of the time, they were trying to gather those who had strayed by their abandonment of the law and their worship of foreign idols and false gods back into the fold of God's chosen people. To re-member in this sense means to bring members back together, to reconnect a people to their membership in the kingdom of God, to recall who they are and to whom they belong. It seems that the goal of the "remember" passages is to bring people back to God, to bring them into closer connection to the LORD.

And yet, right in the middle of all this, Isaiah says "do not remember." Perhaps it would be important to consider the context of this passage and how it relates to the "new thing" that Isaiah speaks of. At the time the latter chapters of Isaiah were written, the Israelites were in exile in Babylon. They had been away from their promised land for generations, long enough that likely most of the original exiled Hebrews had died off, and very few of those still living had memories of anything other than their life in Babylon. To them, the things of old were stories of oppression, injustice, being "other," and not belonging in this land they lived in but was not theirs. Their memories would have been of bitterness, resentment, pain, doubt, and fear. The God of their ancestors must have felt distant and uncaring. Stories of God's saving power expressed in the exodus, the primary narrative of the Hebrew faith, would have had little meaning to them. So what if Moses brought our ancestors out of Egypt! We have been exiled to Babylon, and God has allowed it to happen.

Then, in the midst of this existential angst, God, through Isaiah, says, "Do not remember the former things, or consider the things of old. I am about to do a new thing . . . ." What if God is asking God's people to forget the events of the exile, forget the things they have experienced under Babylonian rule, and to make room instead for God to do a new thing, which is the return from exile? And by extension, what if God is asking the same thing of us? God knows that holding onto any memories that create bitterness and resentment can get in the way of our openness to God's work in our lives. So it makes sense that God would ask us to forget or let go of the "former" things that separate us from God. Perhaps God is calling all of us to let go of the negative memories that prevent us from entering into the "new thing" that God is creating or wants to create in us.

Every clergy person I know has at least one church horror story. To be honest, most have more than one—times when someone in the church they were serving set out on a vicious, unwarranted campaign to get them ousted from the church, times when they were engaged in a bitter conflict with the trustees or mission team or outreach committee over differences in vision, times when a toxic church made every moment of ministry a living hell. Is it possible that any of you are remembering things, people, or events from your ministry that caused you pain, frustration, anger, or doubt? Are you stuck in old hurts or resentments that make you feel far away from God when you want to be closer? Are any of you like Elijah, running away from Jezebel? Are there situations that may have occurred in your churches that contribute to a sense of acedia (spiritual apathy), discouragement, or dissatisfaction with your ministry? Are they blocking your ability to remember God's goodness and mercy? Are these former things getting in the way of fruitfulness, energy, and passion in your work? These painful memories are hard to let go of. They make us sensitive to any behavior or situation that brings back the feelings of those difficult times. And they make it hard for clergy to remember their call and the sense of vision and mission that set them on the path to ministry.

Perhaps it would be good to set aside some time to reflect on your particular stories, maybe even process them with a therapist or spiritual director who can help you gain some perspective on what happened. Ask yourself if these experiences and your feelings about them are interfering with your ability to be in touch with your sense of call as you continue the work of ministry. Then find a way to let go. Some kind of ritual is a good way to do this. When I lead retreats on this topic, I ask retreatants to write a word or two that evoke the situation on a seltzer tablet and drop it into a clear bowl of water, watching it dissolve and disappear. Another possibility is to write down your story as a final purging and then burn it. Pray for God's help in healing from your painful experience and moving on. Make yourself available to the "new thing" God has in store for you.

Remembering Your Call

One of my favorite call narratives in the Hebrew bible is the story of Moses found in Exodus 3 and 4. I love it, because Moses is so deeply *human!* God is calling Moses to something he desperately wants to avoid. Look at the number of excuses he comes up with in his attempts to persuade God that this is a really bad idea. "Who am I to perform such an important task?" "Who *are* you anyway?" "They won't believe me." "I'm a lousy public speaker." "Send someone else!" I also wonder if Moses was considering the fact that he was wanted for murder back in the land of his childhood. If he went to Egypt on this fool's errand—seriously, does God really think that Pharaoh will just let his entire slave force go?—he would most certainly be discovered and executed. But Moses does finally capitulate and follow God's call to a ministry of release for the captives and the leadership of a people who had forgotten who they were and needed to learn how to trust God in all things. This sounds a lot like contemporary ministry to me!

Isaiah's call story, as told in Isaiah 6, bears some similarity to Moses'. It begins with a vision, a burning ember, and self-doubt. Overwhelmed by the vision of God seated on a throne amid the company of heaven, Isaiah realizes his own sinfulness and cries out, "Woe is me . . . for I am a man of unclean lips . . . ."[1] When the seraph touches Isaiah's lips with the burning coal as a purifying act of forgiveness, he is so moved that he gives his life completely over to God, saying, "Here am I. Send me!"[2] It seems to me that this humility is a common response to being called by God for many of the clergy I have known and worked with over the years. The idea that one has been called to ministry is incredibly humbling, and it is good to have these scriptural reminders that God does not call people who are brimming with self-confidence and righteousness. God calls those who are humble enough to lean on the Holy One for strength and wisdom rather than relying on their own resources. God calls ordinary, flawed human beings who are aware of their own weaknesses and are able to look to God for guidance, knowing that the Holy Spirit will equip them for the work of the kingdom.

This equipping work is made clear in both the story of Moses and the call of Jeremiah described in Jeremiah 1:4–10. Again we witness the prophet's powerful vision and the humble protest through Jeremiah's words,

1. Isa 6:5.
2. Isa 6:8b.

"Truly I do not know how to speak; for I am only a boy."[3] It is through God's touch on Jeremiah's lips, and God's reassurance, "Now, I have put my words in your mouth,"[4] that the young prophet is equipped for ministry. God also equipped Moses with the staff that served as a conduit for many miracles throughout the Exodus story. And God's provision of Aaron as a companion and spokesperson, gave Moses strength through all that lay ahead. Through these stories and the prayer offered in Hebrews—"May the God of peace . . . equip you with every good thing to do [God's] will"[5]—clergy can be confident that their needs to do ministry will be supplied.

Take some time to read these call stories in their entirety, listening for words and phrases that arise from the text and upon which you may want to meditate. How do these words speak to you? How do they relate to your own call story? Spend some time reflecting deeply on your call, the feelings you remember from that time, the resistance you may have felt, the humility, power, and overwhelming awe you experienced at being called to do the work of God in the church and in the world. Remember that God is *still* calling you, still equipping you for the work of ministry. Over time, your ministry may have shifted some, or you may feel called to move into a different form of ministry altogether, but the original call is still there, that first pull on your heart to say, "Here I am. Send me."

Remembering Times of Empowerment

In the 1970s, Hungarian psychologist Mihaly Csikszentmihalyi became interested in the phenomenon of "flow," a highly focused mental state experienced by artists and others who become so absorbed in their activity that time, bodily needs, and ego cease to exist. He was inspired by stories of the artist Michelangelo, who supposedly would work on the ceiling of the Sistine Chapel for days without eating or sleeping. He ultimately discovered that many people have this experience of being lost in their work. During research interviews in 1975, several subjects described a feeling during these times of peak performance of being carried along by a current of water, hence the name "flow." Flow is defined as the mental state of operation in which a person engaged in an activity is fully immersed in a feeling of energized focus, full involvement, and success in the process of the activity.

3. Jer 1:6.
4. Jer 1:9.
5. Heb 13:20–21(CEB).

It is a single-minded absorption in an activity that harnesses the emotions for the purpose of performing and learning. In flow, the emotions are not just contained and channeled, but are positive, energized, and aligned with the task at hand. Flow can bring about a feeling of spontaneous joy, or a deep focus in which our awareness is on the task or activity to the exclusion of all else. The experience of flow is not limited to artists, but is experienced by many people in a variety of vocations, including but not limited to athletes, writers, performers, teachers, and certainly clergy.

If you take this psychological, secular term of flow and translate it into sacred terminology, it sounds very much like what people of faith would describe as the action of the Holy Spirit. I think it's safe to say that God empowers God's people through the Holy Spirit. Can you remember times in your ministry when you were in a state of flow, when you felt the power of the Holy Spirit moving through you to accomplish great things? Can you also remember times when you felt blocked, stuck, deflated, and out of touch with God? Sometimes when we are experiencing low energy, self-doubt, or burn-out, it can be helpful to remember the God who empowered the biblical prophets and continues to do so for God's prophets in the church today.

Let's return to the story of Moses for a moment. When God instructed Moses to throw his staff on the ground and turn it into a snake and back again, God showed Moses that he had the ability to perform miracles, to accomplish far more than he could imagine. This was further demonstrated through the transformation of his hand when he put it inside his cloak. These two experiences of the power that God could work through him changed Moses in a very fundamental way. A few chapters later, when he used his staff to turn the Nile into blood in front of the Pharaoh, he was a very different man than the one who resisted God's call with fear and trembling.

The prophetic narrative of Elijah illustrates a number of incidents of empowerment, beginning with the miracle of flour and oil during the great drought recounted in 1 Kings 17. The daily replenishing of ingredients for bread reminds us of the manna God provided in the desert or the feeding of Elijah, the widow, and her son until the famine was over. Empowered by this miracle, Elijah feels enabled to revive the widow's son who has died, throwing his own body over the boy's lifeless one three times until he is revived. As is often the case, small successes lead to bigger successes. With God, there's always more. The empowerment of Elijah culminates in his confrontation with the prophets of Baal in 1 Kings 18. This is the ultimate in flow, in the embodiment of the Holy Spirit. This scene is one of the most dramatic in all of Hebrew scripture—the gauntlet thrown by a defiant Elijah, the bulls on the twin altars, the frantic prayers of the priests of Baal, the drenching of the altar, and the fire called down from heaven. And Elijah, through the Holy Spirit, prevails. What else could have carried him with such confidence through that day?

There are many more stories of empowerment, including Elisha's healing of the water in 2 Kings 2 and Ezekiel's dream of the valley of dry bones in Ezekiel 37, which gave him the confidence to prophecy to the people of Israel who had been exiled in Babylon. You are invited to revisit these narratives and others which may not be mentioned here. Consider the ways in which God's miracles empowered the prophets to do even greater things than they could on their own. Recall your own stories of times when you felt the Spirit moving powerfully in you to further the kingdom. When have you experienced flow? Bringing these memories to mind can remind you of God's presence at the times you needed it most, times when you were aware that without the power of God behind you, you could not have accomplished anything. Remembering can bring you back into a sense of abundant providence and a confidence that can only come from full reliance on God.

Remembering a Sustaining God

Scripture makes it clear that the life of a prophet is one of peril, loneliness, hunger, thirst, and fatigue. Prophets were often ignored, misunderstood, rejected, reviled, ridiculed, and threatened with bodily injury and even death. It's no wonder that none of them were particularly eager to take the job. And yet, time and again, when the prophets were at their lowest point—exhausted, discouraged, and ready to give up—God was there to give them rest, nourishment, encouragement, and sustenance. Throughout the droughts of body, mind, and spirit, God brought refreshment to them.

The most well-known instances of God's sustenance of Moses and the Israelites were the miracles of manna, quail, and water from the rock. Each time the unruly crowd was at the end of their communal rope and threatening to revolt, God provided for their needs in such a way that the people's confidence in Moses was restored.

The prophet Elijah also experienced God's sustaining power in two significant stories from 1 Kings. In the first, Elijah has declared a drought on the land of Ahab, because of his worship of Baal. Wanting to protect Elijah from the drought as well as any possible retribution from the king, God sends Elijah to a ravine east of the Jordan River. There he is attended by ravens that bring him bread and meat both morning and evening. This met his physical needs, but also kept him safe from those who would do him harm. Since ravens normally feed on carrion, the circling flock over Elijah would have indicated to anyone searching for him the presence of a dead carcass and not a live human. In this way, Elijah's hiding place was kept secure until God gave him further instructions and sustenance from another source.

Perhaps the most powerful example of God's sustenance is found in the events immediately following Elijah's defeat of the prophets of Baal. Terrified by the wrath of Jezebel, Elijah's flees across into the desert and collapses near a broom tree, demoralized and not sure if he can go on. Exhausted, he falls into a deep sleep. When he awakens, an angel encourages him to eat and drink of the bread and water provided for him. He sleeps again, and again he awakes to the angel's words, "Get up and eat, otherwise the journey will be too much for you."[6] This gives Elijah the strength to continue to Mount Horeb, where he hears God's voice and is given encouragement and the promise of a companion to walk with him through the next phase of his ministry. In this story, we see that God knows when the journey is too hard, knows when we can't go on without sustenance, and supplies our need for rest, restoration, and renewal. When we are depleted, lonely, and afraid, God brings companions to walk alongside us on this path of ministry.

And so, we have learned that it is by remembering a God who calls, equips, empowers, and sustains that we connect with who we are and what we are called to do and be. The life of ministry is difficult, and certainly there will be days of discouragement and doubt, but when we are grounded in God as the source of all good things, we can be assured that we are never alone. God's faithfulness to God's prophets is unfailing. We can rely on divine providence in every season of ministry to supply what is needed for the work ahead. May it be so.

6. 1 Kgs 19:7b.

Reflection Questions

1. What are the "former things" God is urging you to forget in order to make room for the "new thing" in your life and ministry?

2. As you reflect on your own call story, which of the Biblical stories is most similar to your own? What is the emotional and spiritual impact of remembering your call to ministry?

3. Recall your own stories of empowerment when you experienced "flow" and can now name as the movement of the Holy Spirit working through you. Does this help you have confidence that God is working in your life even when you don't feel it?

4. Which of the Biblical stories of God's sustenance of the prophets do you identify with the most? What is particularly meaningful to you about this passage? What were the divine means by which sustenance was provided? How have you been sustained by God through difficult times? If you are currently in need of sustenance, what person or resource in your life might God use to feed you?

Appendix A

Cognitive Distortions[1]

Filtering: You only notice negative events or thoughts and filter out or dismiss the positive.

All-or-Nothing Thinking: Things are viewed as either black or white, good or bad; there is no middle ground. If you're not perfect, you're a failure. With so much at stake, you must continually defend your point of view to avoid being wrong.

Overgeneralization: You come to a general conclusion based on little or no evidence; one incident is perceived as a never-ending pattern. The words "always" and "never" show up frequently in your thoughts and speech.

Mind Reading: Without their saying so, you think you know what people are thinking and feeling and why they act the way they do. In particular, you make false assumptions about how they feel about you.

Catastrophizing: You expect disaster at every turn. You worry about everything and take precautions that are in excess of actual risk. Your language is full of "what ifs."

Magnification (also called "awfulizing"): Similar to catastrophizing but with a present rather than future focus. You exaggerate current problems and short-comings, characterizing them as horrible or awful. You also believe that you are incapable of handling the problem.

1. Adapted from Burns, *The Feeling Good Handbook,* 1999.

Personalization: You think that everything people do or say is about you and reflects how they feel about you. You also compare yourself to others, often negatively.

Control Fallacies: If you feel controlled by external forces, you view yourself as helpless, a victim of circumstances outside your control. The fallacy of internal control causes you to feel responsible for the pain or happiness of yourself and others.

Fairness Fallacy: When you buy into the belief that life is fair, you become resentful when events or people don't live up to your expectations.

Blaming: You either hold other people responsible for your pain or take the opposite view and blame yourself for everything, when in reality several factors usually contribute to difficulties.

Shoulds: We all grow up with certain values and beliefs about how people should live. For some, these become ironclad rules. When people fail to live up to your set of "shoulds," you become angry, and when you fail to live up to your own standards, you feel guilty.

Labeling: You focus on only one or two qualities of a person or group and turn them into a global negative judgment rather than seeing others as complex, multi-faceted individuals.

Heaven's Reward Fallacy: You expect all your sacrifice and self-denial to pay off through gratitude, acclaim, or reciprocity. You feel bitter when the anticipated reward doesn't come.

Lectio Divina

F rom the time we were in Sunday School, our teachers stressed the need to understand Scripture, to grasp its meaning, or "master" the text. We were trained to memorize important passages. Then, much later, those who felt called to ministry attended seminary where they were taught exegesis—the critical analysis, exposition, or interpretation of Scripture. Again, the purpose is mastery rather than allowing oneself to be shaped spiritually by the Word. But when we approach Scripture from this perspective, we limit God's ability to speak to us in the here and now. The Bible becomes static, linear, and circumscribed, rather than fluid and transcendent.

Through the practice of *Lectio Divina* (Latin for "divine reading") we move from the reading of Scripture as an intellectual pursuit to one of heart and soul. Ancient texts become alive and breathe in and through us. Robert Mulholland writes, "The Word of God is the *action* of the presence, the purpose, and the power of God in the midst of human life."[2] Action implies life and movement. Scripture can be alive and interactive, a book that is still being written today in human hearts that are open to listening to God. I believe that the Bible was not only divinely inspired as it was being written centuries ago, but is divinely inspired still today in the *hearing* of the Word. When we read in the way of *Lectio Divina*, we become the other half of the equation. We receive the Word that was given millennia ago in order to complete the never-ending cycle of giving and receiving that is our relationship with God. When we hear God's word for us, we *become* the Word, so that our lives can serve as a Word God speaks to the world.

Through *Lectio Divina*, instead of reading for information, we read for *formation*. Instead of reading for quantity, we read for *quality*. This

2. Mulholland, *Shaped by the Word*, 41.

might mean only reading a verse or two instead of an entire passage or chapter. We read for depth, not length. Instead of us acting upon the book, the book acts upon us!

Lectio Divina unfolds in four specific movements or steps. The first is *lectio*, or reading. The second is *meditatio*, which means to meditate and reflect on what we have read. *Oratio*, Latin for speech, is our opportunity to respond to the text through prayer, journaling, singing, or any other expression of your response to the passage. Finally, we are invited to *contemplatio*, or contemplation, resting in the text and listening for God's invitation that comes through deep engagement with the Scripture reading.

Appendix C

Spiritual Practice Helps

Prayer for Fellow Travelers on the Road

Lord, you know the thoughts of these,

my companions on the road.

Calm their anxious thoughts,

comfort their painful thoughts,

bless their joyful thoughts,

and guide them safely home.

Amen.

—Sue Magrath

Litany for Meal Preparation

We are blessed when we hunger and thirst for God.

Feed my lambs.

We do not live by bread alone, but by the word of God.

Feed my sheep.

Lord, give us today the bread we need.

Feed my lambs.

Amen.

Scriptures for Household or Outdoor Chores

"Create in me a clean heart, O God, and renew a right spirit within me."
—Ps 51:10

"Wash me, and I will be whiter than snow."
—Ps 51:7b

"Whatever you do, work at it with all your heart, as working for the Lord . . . ."
—Col 3:23

"For we are God's fellow workers; you are God's field, God's building."
—1 Cor 3:9

Walking Prayers

"Let me walk in the way that leads to life."
"I walk in the light of your presence, O Lord."
"Act justly, love mercy, walk humbly with your God."

—Mic 6:8c

Praying the Hours

"Seven times a day do I praise thee because of thy righteous judgments."

—Ps 119:164

Vigils—also known as night watch. Historically, monks rose to pray in the middle of the night. Few of us would choose to embrace this practice now, but for those times when we can't sleep or are awakened in the middle of the night, a prayer of quiet contemplation may still our minds and hearts. Darkness invites a deeper intimacy with God as it conceals the distractions which often draw us away from an attitude of prayer. Use this time to simply be aware of God's presence.

Lauds—also known as morning prayer. This is a time of praise, as God's children celebrate the coming of the light. Spend twenty minutes, if possible, singing a hymn, reading a psalm of praise or other scripture, offering prayers of gratitude, and reciting the Lord's Prayer.

Prime—the beginning of your work day. Take a moment as you review your schedule for the day to pray for God's presence in all that you do. Ask God to sanctify your work and use it for the good of the kingdom.

Terce—mid-morning. For some, this is coffee break time. Use this pause in your work to turn your attention towards God. Breathe slowly and deeply, opening yourself up to God, picturing each breath as an in-filling of the Holy Spirit. Look out a window if you can, and be mindful of God's creation.

Sext—noon, the "hour of illumination." Traditionally, this is a time to pray for peace, as the sun is at its peak, shedding its light on the troubles of the world. Take a moment to pray for those who are most in need of God's help in this hour.

None—mid-afternoon, the winding down of the day. This is a time for taking stock, reviewing your day to see what you have accomplished and what was left undone. As you allow God to be with you in this process, reflect on what you have learned, the times you were nearest to God and the times you acted outside of God's will. Ask for forgiveness and wisdom. Then let go of the day and turn your thoughts toward evening.

Vespers/Compline—a combination of evening and night prayer. As day gives way to night, we turn inward, seeking a place of peace, of quiet surrender to God's love and care. You might spend a few minutes reading from a book on spirituality, then close your day as it began, with a prayer to the Source and Sustainer of life.

Appendix D

Recommended Reading

On Families

Blessed Are the Crazy: Breaking the Silence about Mental Illness, Family, and Church. Sarah Griffith Lund. Atlanta: Chalice, 2014.

I Only Say This Because I Love You: Talking to Your Parents, Partner, Sibs, and Kids When You're All Adults. Deborah Tannen. New York: Ballantine, 2001.

Why Do I Love These People? Po Bronson. London: Random House, 2005.

On Emotional Healing

Don't Forgive Too Soon: Extending the Two Hands That Heal. Dennis Linn, et al. Mahwah, NJ: Paulist, 1997.

The Feeling Good Handbook. David Burns. London: Penguin, 1999.

Forgive & Forget: Healing the Hurts We Don't Deserve. Lewis B. Smedes. London: Harper Collins, 1984.

Forgiveness: The Passionate Journey. Flora Slosson Wuellner. Nashville: Upper Room, 2001.

The Gifts of Imperfection. Brene Brown. Center City, MN: Hazeldon, 2010.

Life After Loss. 6th ed. Bob Deits. Boston: Da Capo Lifelong Books, 2017.

Shame and Grace: Healing the Shame We Don't Deserve. Lewis B. Smedes. London: Harper Collins, 1993.

Where Is God When It Hurts? Philip Yancey. Grand Rapids: Zondervan, 1990.

On Boundaries and Codependency

Codependent No More. Melody Beattie. Center City, MN: Hazeldon, 1986.

Emotional Vampires: Dealing with People Who Drain You Dry. Albert J. Bernstein, Ph.D. London: McGraw-Hill, 2001.

I Don't Have to Make Everything All Better. Gary Lundberg and Joy Lundberg. London: Viking Adult, 1999.

Your Perfect Right: Assertiveness and Equality in Your Life and Relationships. Robert Alberti, Ph.D. and Michael Emmons, Ph.D. 10th ed. Santa Clara, CA: Impact, 2017.

On Healthy Eating

Intuitive Eating. Evelyn Tribole, M.S. and R.D., Elyse Resch, M.S., R.D., F.A.D.A., C.E.D.R.D. 3rd ed. New York: St. Martin's Griffin, 2012.

On Spiritual Practice

An Altar in the World: A Geography of Faith. Barbara Brown Taylor. San Francisco: Harper One, 2009.

A Book of Hours. Thomas Merton, edited by Kathleen Deignan. Notre Dame, IN: Sorin, 2007.

Out of Solitude: Three Meditations on the Christian Life. Henri J. Nouwen. 14th printing. Notre Dame, IN: Ave Maria, 1990.

The Practice of the Presence of God. Brother Lawrence. New Kensington, PA: Whitaker House, 1982.

The Quotidian Mysteries: Laundry, Liturgy and "Women's Work." Kathleen Norris. Mahwah, NJ: Paulist, 1998.

Sacred Necessities: Gifts for Living with Passion, Purpose, and Grace. Terry Hershey. Notre Dame, IN: Sorin, 2005.

Saint Benedict on the Freeway: A Rule of Life for the 21st Century. Corinne Ware. Nashville: Abingdon, 2001.

Seven Sacred Pauses: Living Mindfully through the Hours of the Day. Macrina Wiederkehr. Notre Dame: Sorin, 2008.

Shaped by the Word: The Power of Scripture in Spiritual Formation. M. Robert Mulholland, Jr. Nashville: Upper Room, 2000.

On Wellness and Call

The Cycle of Grace: Living in Sacred Balance. Trevor Hudson, Jerry P. Haas. Nashville: Upper Room, 2012.

Bibliography

The Book of Common Prayer. New York: Penguin, 2012.

Borg, Marcus J. *Convictions: How I Learned What Matters Most.* New York: HarperOne, 2014.

Brown, Brene. *The Gifts of Imperfection: Let Go of Who You Think You're Supposed to Be and Embrace Who You Are.* Center City, MN: Hazelden, 2010.

Burns, David D. *The Feeling Good Handbook.* New York: Penguin, 1999.

Dickerson, Jim. "The Political and Social Dimensions of Embodied Christian Contemplative Prayer." In *Reclaiming the Body in Christian Spirituality,* edited by Thomas Ryan, 116–52. New York: Paulist, 2004.

Driskill, Joseph D. "Spiritual Direction with Traumatized Persons." In *Still Listening: New Horizons in Spiritual Direction,* edited by Norvene Vest, 17–36. Harrisburg, PA: Morehouse, 2000.

Eck, Diana L. *Encountering God.* Boston: Beacon, 2003.

Gauger, Robert, and Leo Christie. *Clergy Stress and Depression.* Professional Development Resources, www.pdresources.org, 2013.

Guenther, Margaret. *Holy Listening: The Art of Spiritual Direction.* Cambridge, MA: Cowley, 1992.

Halloran, Kevin. "D. L. Moody Quotes: Inspiring Quotations by Dwight L. Moody," accessed April 2019. www.kevinhalloran.net/d-l-moody-quotes/.

Hershey, Terry. *Sacred Necessities: Gifts for Living with Passion, Purpose, and Grace.* Notre Dame, IN: Sorin, 2005.

Job, Rueben P., and Norman Shawchuck. *A Guide to Prayer for All Who Seek God.* Nashville: Upper Room, 2003.

Kidd, Sue Monk. *Firstlight.* New York: Guideposts, 2006.

Landreth, Garry L. *Play Therapy: The Art of the Relationship.* 3rd ed. New York: Routledge, 2012.

Linn, Dennis, et al. *Don't Forgive Too Soon: Extending the Two Hands That Heal.* New York: Paulist, 1997.

London, H. B., Jr., and N. B. Wiseman. *Pastors at Greater Risk.* Ventura, CA: Regal, 2003.

The Merriam-Webster Dictionary. Springfield, MA: Merriam-Webster, 1997.

Merton, Thomas. *A Book of Hours.* Edited by Kathleen Deignan. Notre Dame, IN: Sorin, 2007.

———. *Seeds.* Edited by Robert Inchausti. Boston: Shambhala, 2002.

Mulholland, M. Robert. *Shaped by the Word: The Power of Scripture in Spiritual Formation.* Nashville: Upper Room, 2000.

Norris, Kathleen. *The Quotidian Mysteries: Laundry, Liturgy and "Women's Work."* New York: Paulist, 1998.

Nouwen, Henri J. M. *Life of the Beloved: Spiritual Living in a Secular World.* New York: Crossroad, 1992.

———. *Out of Solitude.* Notre Dame, IN: Ave Maria, 1990.

O'Donohue, John. *Anam Cara: A Book of Celtic Wisdom.* New York: Cliff Street, 1997.

Paintner, Christine Valtars. *Eyes of the Heart: Photography as a Christian Contemplative Practice.* Notre Dame, IN: Sorin, 2013.

Palmer, Parker J. *Let Your Life Speak: Listening for the Voice of Vocation.* San Francisco: Jossey-Bass, 2000.

Parks, Sharon Daloz, et al. *Common Fire: Leading Lives of Commitment in a Complex World.* Boston: Beacon, 1997.

Peck, M. Scott. *The Road Less Traveled: A New Psychology of Love, Traditional Values and Spiritual Growth.* New York: Touchstone, 1978.

Rupp, Joyce. *Out of the Ordinary: Prayers, Poems, and Reflections for Every Season.* Notre Dame, IN: Ave Maria, 2000.

Ryan, Thomas. "Toward a Positive Spirituality of the Body." In *Reclaiming the Body in Christian Spirituality,* edited by Thomas Ryan, 21–56. New York: Paulist, 2004.

Shockley, Donald G. *Private Prayers in Public Places: The Notebook of an Urban Pilgrim.* New York: iUniverse, 2004.

Steindl-Rast, Brother David. *Gratefulness, the Heart of Prayer: An Approach to Life in Fullness.* New York: Paulist, 1984.

Taylor, Barbara Brown. *An Altar in the World: A Geography of Faith.* New York: HarperOne, 2009.

Watterson, Bill. "Calvin and Hobbes." Comic strip in *Alive Now,* July/August 2007, 24.

———. *The Days Are Just Packed.* Kansas City, MO: Andrews and McMeel, 1993.

Wikiquote. "Menachem Mendel of Kotzk," accessed April 2019. https://en.wikiquote.org/wiki/Meachem_Mendel_of_Kotzk.

Wiseman, James. "The Body in Spiritual Practice: Some Historical Points of Reference." In *Reclaiming the Body in Christian Spirituality,* edited by Thomas Ryan, 1–20. New York: Paulist, 2004.

Wuellner, Flora Slosson. *Forgiveness, the Passionate Journey: Nine Steps of Forgiving through Jesus' Beatitudes.* Nashville: Upper Room, 2001.

Yaconelli, Michael. *Dangerous Wonder: The Adventure of Childlike Faith.* Colorado Springs: NavPress, 2003.